Memory
Power

This Large Print Book carries the
Seal of Approval of N.A.V.H.

Memory Power

You Can Develop a Great Memory
— America's Grand Master
Shows You How

Scott Hagwood

Thorndike Press • Waterville, Maine

Published in 2006 by arrangement with Free Press,
a division of Simon & Schuster Inc.

Thorndike Press® Large Print Health, Home & Learning.

The tree indicium is a trademark of Thorndike Press.

The text of this Large Print edition is unabridged.
Other aspects of the book may vary from the original edition.

Set in 16 pt. Plantin by Elena Picard.

Printed in the United States on permanent paper.

Library of Congress Cataloging-in-Publication Data

Hagwood, Scott.
    Memory power : you can develop a great memory —
America's grand master shows you how / by Scott Hagwood.
  — Large print ed.
     p. cm. — (Thorndike Press large print health, home,
learning)
    ISBN 0-7862-8563-X (lg. print : hc : alk. paper)
    1. Mnemonics. 2. Large type books. I. Title. II. Series.
BF385.H245 2006b
   153.1′4—dc22   2006002056

Memory Power

As the Founder/CEO of NAVH, the only national health agency solely devoted to those who, although not totally blind, have an eye disease which could lead to serious visual impairment, I am pleased to recognize Thorndike Press* as one of the leading publishers in the large print field.

Founded in 1954 in San Francisco to prepare large print textbooks for partially seeing children, NAVH became the pioneer and standard setting agency in the preparation of large type.

Today, those publishers who meet our standards carry the prestigious "Seal of Approval" indicating high quality large print. We are delighted that Thorndike Press is one of the publishers whose titles meet these standards. We are also pleased to recognize the significant contribution Thorndike Press is making in this important and growing field.

Lorraine H. Marchi, L.H.D.
Founder/CEO
NAVH

* Thorndike Press encompasses the following imprints: Thorndike, Wheeler, Walker and Large Print Press.

Contents

Introduction 9

1 Meeting My Memory 19

2 The "Write" Way to Remember   48

3 Making Sense of Our Senses . . . 73

4 Association and Interest 92

5 The Art and Science
    of Repetition 112

6 Discovering the Roman Room . 137

7 Remembering Names
    and Faces 161

8 Memory Enemies 197

9 An Amazing Discovery 221

10 Putting Your Memory
    to Work 239

11 The Memory Gym 265

    Appendix
    The Rules of the
        Memory Competition 297

    Acknowledgments 325

Introduction

I know, you think you have a lousy memory. You can't find your car keys, you forgot to send that e-mail yesterday, or maybe, worse, you forgot your anniversary!

Relax; your memory is just fine. I can almost guarantee it. For years I was in the same boat you think you're in. I was a mediocre student. I suffered the acute embarrassment of forgetting, in front of an audience, how to play a simple piano piece. I couldn't remember where I put my car keys. And then I found out I had cancer.

What does having cancer have to do with memory? The doctors told me the treatment that I would undergo would have an effect on my brain that would make it difficult for me to concentrate and remember. There's the ultimate insult: Add to the terror of having a life-threatening disease a treatment that makes my already forgetful memory worse! I had to leave my treatment to the doctors — and they did a wonderful job — but I decided that I could do something at least to mitigate the effects of the treatment on my brain. If you had told me five years ago that I would hold the title of National Memory Champion, I would have laughed out loud. Not a chance! I was just an average guy doing my best to get through life while enjoying my wife and children. But I won the national championships in four consecutive years. How I succeeded in doing that is what this book is all about.

I discovered that a person's memory is much like his or her body. Exercise it and it gets stronger. The trick lies in knowing how to do the exercises. In *Memory Power* I'll show you how to do exercises for your memory. And the best part is that you'll find the exercises amazingly easy, yet they yield powerful results. Within a week you'll find yourself remembering more and using those memories to make your life better.

Cancer is a life-altering experience for anyone who has the disease. Chapter 1 is about how my brush with death taught me that everybody has far more memory potential than they realize. Fortunately, my cancer was curable and I had a wonderful team of doctors to whom I'll always be grateful. As I was undergoing the frightening treatment regimen the doctors laid out, I struggled to keep my thinking and memory intact. I was fearful that I would lose some vital part of what made me the person I was. Then, in something of a revelation, I discovered that I had a great memory! I could remember tiny details of events that happened years ago. While the treatments took a temporary toll on my ability to concentrate and remember things that happened minutes earlier, I reveled in the knowledge of what I *did* remember. How, I wondered, was it possible to have such vivid recall of long-ago events? And that set me off on the course of discovery and learning that I'm sharing with you. You won't believe how amazing your mind and memory are until you experience this. You'll have to take my word for it now, but you'll be a believer in just a few days.

We'll start your exercise program in chapter 2. Think of it as sort of a warm-up. All it really consists of is keeping a daily journal, jotting down at the end of the day some of the things that happened to you — people you met, decisions you made, even what you had for lunch. It doesn't take long to do. Then we'll examine what your journal reveals about how you remember and take a few basic steps to improve on that process. We aren't going to engage in any "tricks." This is all stuff you're already doing without realizing it.

After warming up, we'll explore in chapter 3 the ways in which memories are made. There are two ways to look at the process of memory. One is what you would call scientific and involves neurons, dendrites, chemicals, and electricity in a complex process that we'll leave mostly to the scientists. The other way to view memory is as the result of your senses, emotions, and actions at work. A memory is the result of an experience, and we experience the world around us through our five senses: seeing, hearing, feeling, tasting, and smelling. Our emotions play a role, too, since we usually have negative or positive reactions to experiences. Finally, many experiences we have involve action. We act or are acted upon or maybe we just imagine an action. Combine these ingredients — our senses, emotions, and actions — and you have a memory! You're already doing all of this, of course, but mostly without thinking about it. The point of chapter 3 and the exercises in it is to get you to do more thinking about your experiences in order to form more exacting and fulfilling memories.

You probably won't be surprised to learn

that human beings tend to best remember things that interest them. Chapter 4 shows you how to use that common trait to build more complete memories. In essence, you'll learn to associate whatever you wish or need to remember with something that interests you. It's the simple principle of connectivity — everything can be connected in some fashion to everything else. You'll find that your brain is capable of some very creative ways to connect things. Much of the process of association involves the creation of mental pictures. Again, you do this all the time without realizing it. Hear the word *breakfast* and your mind's eye conjures up something associated with breakfast, maybe scrambled eggs on a plate or the smell of sausage cooking. These mental images will become another of the tools you use to focus your memory.

In chapter 5 we're going to learn about the role of repetition in memory enhancement. I know what you're thinking: Here's the tough part where I have to keep repeating stuff over and over until I have it memorized. Wrong! It's very unfortunate that so many people think that endless repetition is the key to memory. The real key to repetition in memory is that it's more like planting seeds. You plant the memory once, then come back every so often to cultivate and nourish it. Time is a powerful eraser trying to rid you of your memories. But by using the tools we've already assembled, you'll learn in chapter 4 how to form and store memories most efficiently and to protect them from time's decay.

Now that we have a solid framework for forming memories, we come in chapter 6 to an amazing memory technique that was invented thousands of years ago but fell into disuse for centuries. It's called the Roman Room and I find it the single most important tool in memorizing anything. It basically teaches you to use the structure of almost any room — four walls, four corners, a floor and ceiling — to store and recall your memories. Roman Rooms are eternal forget-me-not spots that are adaptable to any kind of information and serve to build bridges between your working memory and your long-term memory. The process is the same no matter what you want to remember. As I've developed my memory, one of the things that has amazed me is that the *process* of remembering can be so fascinating. People sometimes ask me how I keep from becoming bored when I'm preparing for a memory competition by memorizing decks of cards. Of course, over the years I've remembered countless thousands of cards in practice. Yet, when I get to the end of the very next deck, I'm still amazed at my ability to remember. It's an insatiable feeling. The Roman Room acts as a gateway to your permanent storage area, allowing you to easily transfer information that would otherwise be lost to an area that has unlimited storage capacity. Although all memory is subject to the whitewash of time, the Roman Room acts as a buffer between the newly stored information and time's obsessive compulsion to cleanse your mental hard drive. I know it sounds strange, but just wait until you try it!

Probably the most embarrassing aspect of memory is forgetting someone's name. The problem is often that introductions happen too quickly. It's not that you are getting too much information, you're just getting it too quickly. In chapter 7 we'll get into some strategies and secrets for remembering names, ranging from paying closer attention when we're being introduced to someone to associating some facet of a person with a similar facet of someone we already know. The exercises in this chapter are easy and fun. You can do them by looking through your old high-school yearbook, or practice them each time you visit Wal-Mart or Home Depot. You can even use newspaper ads and The Weather Channel to hone your ability to recall names.

No matter how well trained your memory may be, there will be occasions when it just doesn't work as well as you would like. We already know that time is a powerful enemy of memory, but there are three others that are just as bad: stress, lack of sleep, and not paying attention. Chapter 8 is all about how to recognize and combat these enemies. We'll also learn to reconstruct memories that might have fallen victim to these devious enemies.

In chapter 9 we'll visit The Discovery Channel and a team of brain researchers who want to take a look at my brain at work. While what they find is interesting in and of itself, what I really want you to take away from this chapter is the feeling that "If this guy Hagwood can do this, so can I." Because that's the truth.

What you may not realize is that the skills you develop to improve your memory are transferable and so can be used in every part of your life, from improving your career to improving your social life. That's what chapter 10 is all about. What it all boils down to is that improving your memory improves your ability to think. I think you'll enjoy seeing how the events that comprise the National Memory Championships — events that might at first seem silly or useless to you — can have practical applications in your life.

We'll wrap up our journey to a more powerful memory in The Memory Gym. Based on the text you'll be reading, I've prepared seven exercises, one for each day of the week, that will give your memory a significant boost. Of course, you can do them at whatever pace suits you. If you find they're helpful, they can easily be adapted to become memory workouts for the rest of your life.

The past five years have been an incredible journey for me. If your improved memory gives you a fraction of the satisfaction and joy that I've gained, you'll have had an incredible journey, too.

Chapter One
Meeting My Memory

The dreaded words came on January 14, 1999, my thirty-sixth birthday.

"Scott, it's cancer and it has spread. We need to do the surgery right away, today."

I had been praying that the biopsy Dr. James Thomas had done the day before would show that the little lump on my thyroid gland, discovered several weeks earlier during my first physical examination in eighteen years, was a benign nodule. Before the biopsy Dr. Thomas had told me that some people choose to go ahead and remove the entire thyroid during the biopsy procedure, but he wanted to avoid that if he could. A person can live very well without a thyroid, but the absence of the gland requires a lifetime regimen of drug therapy.

Now there was no choice. During the second surgery Dr. Thomas removed my thyroid as well as a suspicious lump in an adjacent lymph node. His skill spared me any damage to my vocal cords and the scar would be practically invisible.

A week later I was back in his office, where he inspected the incision and nodded approval at the rapid healing. But then his tone turned somber.

"I believe we got it all," he said. "But the problem with this type of cancer is that it can come back. Even though we cleaned up everything we could find around your gland, it's likely that small bits of thyroid tissue, some too small for us to retrieve, are still present. If so, there could be micro-tumors within the tissue that could come back. Studies indicate that there's a 30 percent rate of return, but it's up to you to decide if you want additional treatment. I can go ahead now and start you on Synthroid, the drug you'll take for the rest of your life. But if you decide you want additional therapy, I need to delay the Synthroid to avoid drug interactions."

I wasn't ready for this. I was just weaning myself from the pain medication, I felt terrible, and the last thing I wanted to do was research treatments and calculate odds, especially when I was gambling with my life. But my wife, Janet, was way ahead of me, as usual. She already had contacted Dr. Joseph Moore, an oncologist at Duke University Hospital who had worked with her father's cancer for years. Dr. Moore was unequivocal: Take the additional treatment.

Since the initial discovery of the lump during my physical, I'd learned a lot about the thyroid gland. I had already known, of course, that it affected heart rate and metabolism and that people with thyroid problems often felt tired. But I learned that the effects of the thyroid hormone are far more extensive, affecting every cell in the body, facilitating all the physical and chemical processes that allow cell growth and maintain body functions. Most worrisome to me was that a lack of thyroxin often results in difficulty in focusing and concentrating and sometimes produces severe memory loss. But the doctors were reassuring: Once the right level of synthetic thyroxin is found by trial and error, those effects usually disappear.

The additional treatment would require about three weeks and they would be some of the most bizarre and traumatic of my life. Dr. Moore explained the process: "We need to destroy any remnants of thyroid tissue. The thyroid gland naturally attracts iodine in your bloodstream. Therefore, you are going to swallow a solution of radioactive iodine that will seek and destroy thyroid tissue, kind of like a submarine mission in those old World War II movies. However, your body will become radioactive. Your progress will be measured with a Geiger counter and you'll be confined to a lead-lined room for a couple of days. Although your body will rid itself of most of the radiation through your urine and sweat, you will still have trace amounts of the material in your body for up to three weeks. Whatever you bring into the lead-lined room stays in the room — books, papers, whatever. So don't bring any laptops or other valuables."

"Why?" I asked. "If there are only going to be trace amounts in my sweat glands, what would it matter?"

"That's *after* the two days you're inside the room. While you're in the room you'll be hot enough that people will have only limited contact with you and will wear badges to monitor radiation when they do. Anything you touch will be contaminated. You will be given a list of the protocols and all your questions will be answered, so be sure to write them all down so you don't forget."

Thankfully, he winked when he said that.

I felt well enough to go to the local

bookstore to browse through books about the brain and how it works. I wanted to see if there was anything proactive I could do to mitigate the loss of memory and other cognitive skills. One of the many books I thumbed through was *Use Your Perfect Memory*, by Tony Buzan. The jacket copy described Buzan as "one of the world's leading authorities on the brain and learning techniques." One passage particularly caught my attention:

"I remember at least three students during my undergraduate years who knew more about certain subjects than practically everyone else in our classes and who consequently used to give private tutoring and coaching to those who were struggling. Extraordinarily, these bright students would regularly fail to excel at examination time, invariably complaining that they had not had enough time in the examination room to gather together the mass of knowledge that they had and that for some reason they 'forgot' at critical moments."

That's just like me, I thought. I studied hard in school but often did poorly on tests.

Then I read an exercise that Buzan had developed using a deck of cards to improve your memory. I didn't fully understand how it worked, but I knew I would soon have plenty of time on my hands and taking a cheap deck of cards into the lead-lined room was no big loss. I bought the book.

My session in the lead room was scheduled for three weeks later. As I waited to begin the therapy, my life slowly descended into a surreal, sluggish world. Deprived of my thyroid gland's steady supply of thyroxin, I found that everything became much more difficult. Most people read for relaxation. I became physically and mentally exhausted after reading just a few pages, and nothing stuck in my memory. I simply couldn't make sense of what I read. And my verbal skills suffered just as badly. If someone asked me a question, I would start to answer, then completely lose my train of thought. I often wondered if this was what Alzheimer's was like — aware one moment and not the next.

On February 19, 1999, I took my first full dose of radioactive medicine to destroy the remnants of cancer floating inside my throat. The hospital room seemed ordinary enough except for the door. It looked like the entrance to a bank vault. A nurse brought me the radioactive iodine solution in what looked like a Stone Age soup can, the kind Fred Flintstone might use, chiseled out of rock and heavy as hell. Janet had just left the room. Inside the heavy can was a small vial of what looked like clear water. I was relieved that it wasn't glowing. As instructed, I drank it, then washed it down with several cups of water. It tasted warm and bland. I wondered if the warmth had anything to do with its nuclear nature.

As the nurse left, the closing door thudded with the heaviness of a stone being rolled against a tomb. Oddly, the deafening silence suddenly reminded me of my first and only piano recital. The clarity of that memory was surprisingly perfect. It was as if I had been transported back in time.

My recital piece, "Skater's Waltz" — a very streamlined adaptation of the classic composition — was designed to demonstrate what meager skills I had developed as a reluctant pianist. I had spent countless hours banging away on our family piano in the living room, memorizing the string of notes. On the dreaded day of the recital, the small gathering of proud parents and obligated siblings might as well have been a crowd of thousands. The dozen or so student performers were sequestered in a small room offstage, a breeding ground of nervous anticipation that grew into primal fear. My hands and legs were shaking. The applause awarded to the younger students did nothing to calm me. My hands and legs would not stop shaking. Strangely, my mind filled with images of the joys of speeding down wet streets on my bike, then slamming on the brakes and sliding to a stop. Would my fingers slip off the piano keys as easily as my bicycle tires slipped on wet pavement?

Finally, the moment arrived. My teacher introduced me. For a moment I stood stock-still, unable to leave the anonymous safety of backstage. Then I stumbled toward the baby grand piano. I didn't look at the audience but kept my gaze fixed on the black and white keys. Surely they would restore my depleted confidence and drain the trembling from my hands. I thought I had become good friends with those eighty-eight keys during the months of practicing. But the moment I placed my fingers in the beginning position, they betrayed me. I realized that I had never played on this particular piano before. I froze. The keys somehow seemed longer and more elegant, with a kind of majestic shine that was different from the upright piano at home. It felt different. I was paralyzed. The silence was smothering, like an invisible blanket of fog that reduced my vision to the taunting keys in front of me. Everything else blurred into a haze that quickly penetrated my brain and erased "Skater's Waltz" from my mind.

I don't know how long I sat there. Then came the voice of my best friend's mother, Jean-Ann Livesay: "You can do it, Scotty!" Those wonderful words that broke the silence in the room also broke the frozen grip of fear on my body. But the result was no better. I stood up, turned to the expectant audience, and mumbled, "Ladies and gentlemen, I forgot my piece."

I slunk off the stage, desperate for the solace of the green room, only to find that the other students were taking especially malevolent delight in my failed performance. I never took another piano lesson.

This memory flashed across my mind in the instant the lead door closed. I could almost feel the piano keys as I looked at my fingers and thought about my sweaty hands. In a moment of black humor, I wanted to will myself back in time and play "Skater's Waltz," contaminating those traitorous keys with radioactive sweat.

That's when it hit me: I could remember

27

the past with virtually perfect clarity! I might not be able to concentrate in the present, but clearly my long-term memory was functioning perfectly. The speed and detail of my piano-recital recollection was staggering given my state of mental sluggishness. No effort had been required to retrieve the information. It had come automatically.

Suddenly, some of the things Tony Buzan described in his book began to make sense. I had never thought about this before. In order to unlock the secret of remembering a deck of cards with lightning speed, I needed to discover how I naturally collected and stored memories.

Cancer is always a life-altering event, for better or worse, for its victims. That dreaded phone call on my thirty-sixth birthday signaled the beginning of a journey that would take me to the lowest point of my mental and physical life. And although the cancer destroyed my thyroid gland, it also opened the door to an appreciation of the reliability, necessity, and accuracy of human memory. This book is about what I learned on that extraordinary journey and how you can apply it to improve your own memory.

The Bad Memory Poster Child

Many of us go through life convinced that we don't have a very good memory. How many times have you heard this comment or something like it: "Honey, have you seen the car keys? I don't remember where I put them." And how many times have you run into that neighbor in the grocery store and for the life of you couldn't remember her name? Have you ever thought you're subject to any of the following conditions?

- I have difficulty comprehending.
- I have a short attention span.
- I'm terrible with names.
- I'm easily bored.
- I do poorly on tests.

Don't worry: We've all felt at least a few of those notions. The proliferation over the past decade of Post-it notes and over the last few years of Palm Pilots attest to our attempt to get things done that we fear we will otherwise forget. Bill Cosby, the comedian, likes to describe his "Memory Is in the Butt Theory." He sometimes walks into a room and forgets why he's there.

When that happens, he retreats to the room he just left, sits down, and then usually he remembers what he wanted to do in that other room.

Those of us who are around young children often notice how they have only to see or hear things once to be able to stow that information away in their minds. We marvel at the power of young minds being formed and are reminded at the same time that we aren't getting any younger. We unconsciously conclude that memory is a transient gift for the young, which erodes as we age.

When I was young I could have qualified as the poster boy for bad memory. Going to school in the 1970s in the foothills of Tennessee near the Great Smoky Mountains, I thought that "memory" was just a convenient way to describe the boring, rote repetition of facts or figures that eventually dug a trench in my brain like the grooves of the ancient 33 rpm records that my third-grade teacher made me use to learn my multiplication tables. I can still hear the sound of that monotone female voice droning over and over: "Three times two is six, three times three is nine, three times four is twelve." Much of school seemed geared toward relentless repetition. Learning to write involved hours and hours of practice repeating letters again and again until they were perfect. Even more advanced subjects like algebra and geometry involved working the same kinds of problems over and over again until a mind-numbing pattern formed in my head.

I did manage to learn some mnemonic tricks that helped a little. The acronym HOMES allowed me to whip off the names of the Great Lakes easily: Huron, Ontario, Michigan, Erie, and Superior. In science class I managed to recall the organization of living things with the sentence King Philip Came Over For Good Spaghetti (Kingdom, Phylum, Class, Order, Family, Genus, and Species). The planets orbiting the sun were identified by this carefully crafted sentence: My Very Educated Mother Just Served Us Nine Pizzas (Mercury, Venus, Earth, Mars, Jupiter, Saturn, Uranus, Neptune, and Pluto).

Often, though, my little tricks didn't stand up to the rigors of exams. My memory had an annoying habit of blanking under the stress of a test. Did my very educated mother order pizzas or spaghetti? Like an Etch A Sketch drawing that disappears when shaken, my ability to recall information seemed to dissipate after being jarred by the first few questions. As a result, I didn't perform well in class and, compared to my friends, I felt stupid. That belief was reinforced when I graduated low in my high school class and my SATs were just above the minimum needed to be accepted into the University of Tennessee.

College was even worse than high school, especially since I chose to study engineering. And not just any engineering, but chemical engineering, arguably one of the most difficult undergraduate degrees to obtain. I'd like to say I chose that major because I recognized my scholastic shortcomings and believed that such a difficult degree would provide the challenge I needed to unlock my mental potential. But other reasons were at work. Partly, it was peer pressure. I thought that if I chose a tough degree, that would somehow make up for my lack of great grades and I could still be included "in the group." But the main reason I chose it was that my father is an engineer and I didn't want to disappoint him by pursuing some other degree. Of course I recognize the near insanity of that decision today. In high school, my worst grades were in chemistry and I hated it. Maybe it was some kind of teenage madness, that transient affliction of virtually all people between the ages of thirteen and nineteen that makes them believe they are invincible. That state of mind lives for the thrill of the moment — "Dad, I've decided to become a chemical engineer" — with no thought for the long-term consequences. My decision opened a Pandora's box of misery for the next five years.

I struggled in college. I pounded away at my mental keys many a late night, trying to imprint information on my brain just long enough to pass the tests. Amazingly, the freshman "weed-out" classes designed to make victims of people like me didn't do their job. But at the beginning of my junior year, after officially declaring my final major, I spectacularly failed a crucial chemistry exam that jeopardized all the work I had put in thus far. I'll never forget the disgusted look on the professor's face when he tossed the dreaded blue book at me with a big red 6 (out of a possible score of 100) circled on the front cover. This failure became a critical point in my life that not only fueled doubts about my memory but called into question my intellectual ability to complete the degree.

Stress, pressure, exam anxiety, lack of

sleep, and a profound ignorance of natural learning styles left me with a very poor opinion of my memory. Although I wanted to hold on to the belief that my true intelligence was not reflected in my grades, such consistent mediocre performance made it a strain to keep up my confidence. Learning and school had become something to be endured. I never gave any thought to memory improvement — college had become simply a matter of survival. And, to add another black layer to my already dim perception of my mental abilities, I just assumed that the widely held view that memory grew worse with age was true. By default, I assumed that a good memory is something that a person is born with or not. I had heard the term *photographic memory* but I thought that any such ability was a blessing granted by the cosmic stork. He forgot to include it in the little bundle of joy that was me.

You Can Read This Line, Can't You?

You're probably convinced that you have a bad memory. Why else would you be reading a book about improving your memory? But let's take a minute to ponder a few things. Do you know what a ringing telephone sounds like? Do you know how an onion tastes? Do you recognize your spouse's face?

Of course you do. Those are all things you've experienced in the past and you're now recalling them with perfect clarity. If you have such a bad memory, how can you recall those things — and uncountable other sounds, tastes, smells, and sights — so well? Here's an even bigger revelation: The fact that you're able to read this book attests to the incredible power of your memory. This book is composed of words that in turn are composed of letters. There are billions of possible combinations of letters to make into words, words into sentences, sentences into paragraphs, and paragraphs into books or articles. Yet most of us are able to breeze right through a book or magazine article without ever consciously thinking about those manifold ways of putting it all together. We simply have perfect recall of the patterns of letters that form words and can assimilate huge amounts of information from those words without even trying.

Since I became recognized as something of a memory expert, I've had many people tell me that while they have a bad memory, they have experienced incidents of amazing memory. My good friend Andy Foley had a hamburger at lunch recently that reminded him of a similar hamburger he'd had back in the sixth grade. "It was like I was transported back in time," he told me. "I could see the details of the lunchroom, the menu, the countertop, and even hear some of the conversations around me. I could even remember how I was feeling. It was a powerful experience."

Another friend, an architect, complains that he constantly has to refer back to the local building codes to ensure that his plans are in compliance. He'll think the particular standard he wants to check is in chapter 18 of the code, only to discover that it's in chapter 5. "That happens all the time," he says. "Yet I can remember the batting average of every New York Yankee from 2001 until now."

Strange, isn't it, the way memory seems to work? There are so many things we can remember with perfect clarity and no effort, while other things simply refuse to take up lodging in our brain. We can turn to science for some explanations, although you may be surprised to learn how much science doesn't know about memory. Focused scientific inquiry into the nature of memory is in its infancy. But, propelled by the enormous toll that Alzheimer's disease and other dementias are taking on our population, funding is increasing rapidly and more of the best scientific minds are turning their efforts to understanding memory. It's encouraging that the recipients of the 2004 Nobel Prize in Medicine were two researchers who determined that the brain, working through the nose, can distinguish and remember ten thousand different odors. The researchers — Linda Buck and Richard Axel — have concluded that the brain is wired to instantly recall odors as either positive or negative experiences. The smell of smoke, for instance, can elicit a warning signal, while the scent of a ripe strawberry can trigger an intense desire for a big hunk of luscious strawberry shortcake.

A Mercifully Quick Chemistry Lesson

Each time we learn something we create a web of experience using thousands of brain cells, or neurons, that come together like pieces of a jigsaw puzzle to form a picture or an experience. It is the pattern of those pieces that makes the memory. Our brains are composed of 100 billion neurons, individual powerhouses of chemical and electrical energy that are about one hundred times smaller than the width of a human hair. Curiously, each neuron has a phobia: It doesn't want to be touched. There is a small gap about one-millionth of an inch wide, called the synapse, that separates each neuron from the next.

A typical neuron consists of three primary components. The principal fiber, called the axon, sends information to other neurons. The dendritic spines receive information from other neurons, and the dendrites carry the new information from the dendritic spines to the cell body. You might picture a neuron looking a little like a plucked dandelion in the spring. The hollow stem would be the axon. Change the big puffy white seed heads into rubbery strings jutting out in every direction and you have the dendrites. The frayed-looking ends of those rubbery strings would be the dendritic spines.

Information from the cell body is carried down through the axon by electrical energy. The electrical charge then stimulates a sac full of chemicals called neurotransmitters that flood the gap between the axon of one neuron and the dendritic spine of another, creating a chemical and electrical connection between the two cells, but not a physical connection. The second neuron converts the information it received from the first neuron via the chemical release and then converts it to electrical energy, which in turn fires a connection with a third neuron, and so on. Although a neuron has only one axon, it has up to ten thousand dendrites and even more dendritic spines. Research studies suggest that one neuron can be connected to ten thousand other neurons and each of those neurons connected up to another ten thousand neurons. Keep making those connections and pretty soon you have a vastly complex superhighway of information capable of storing enormous amounts of data and recalling it almost instantly. It's been estimated that the storage capacity of the human brain is nearly infinite. During your lifetime, your brain will have stored more information than five times the amount of total printed material in the world, or more than fifty thousand times the amount of text contained in the U.S. Library of Congress. And you thought the Internet was awesome!

Memories arise when the firing of neurons creates a pattern similar to one that has occurred before. That pattern is called a memory trace. Neuroscientists like to say that "neurons that fire together wire together." So when one fires, they all fire, recreating the initial pattern that generates the memory of an event.

With all that firing and connecting going on, you might wonder if learning and memory increase the physical size of your brain. According to studies conducted on London taxi drivers, who have highly developed spatial skills that enable them to easily maneuver around the complicated streets of the city, the answer is yes. The hippocampus, a seahorse-shaped structure located in the limbic system of the brain, is responsible for transferring working memory to long-term memory. In London's taxi drivers, the hippocampus tends to be larger than it is in control subjects. Another study, in Germany, showed that people who studied how to juggle for three months showed an increase in gray matter in regions of the brain responsible for visual and motor activity.

The pathways between cells are created by stimuli that come from our various senses: sight, hearing, touch, smell, and taste. Any one of those senses can create a memory. But it really gets interesting when two or more senses are involved simultaneously. Dr. Paul Laurienti, an associate professor at Wake Forest University Medical Center, described it to me this way:

"If I were to just see a fire engine — not hear it, but just see it — the sight would affect an area in the back of my brain about the size of a quarter. Now, if I were just to hear a fire engine, not see it, the sound would affect an area in my brain located just over the left ear, about the size of a fifty-cent piece. But if I were to both see and hear a fire engine, not only would both areas of the brain operate, but each area would expand." Think of it: Instead of 75 cents' worth of memory, we actually get about 85 cents' worth of memory. And that's with only two senses being involved. Dr. Laurienti said that research proves that as more and more senses are activated, there is an ever-increasing activation in the brain that subsequently increases our natural ability to remember. It isn't often that we go through our day with just two senses operating, so think about the possibilities of enhancing our brain just through the process of living.

One of the most fascinating experiences of my life was to have my brain observed by Functional Magnetic Resonance Imaging (fMRI) technology while I was undertaking a rigorous exercise in memory power. I fully expected the film of that session to show my brain ablaze with activity as I focused on the exercise. Instead, the fMRI showed my brain just loafing along. I'll tell you more about that experience later in the book, but let me just make this one point about that fMRI exam: The more you exercise your brain, the more efficient it becomes at processing information. What science is telling us is that having a fantastic memory isn't the result of some gift from birth. Anyone can have a great memory. It's just a matter of learning how to train it and use it. If I can do it, you can do it.

Improve Your Memory, Improve Your Life

Obviously you have some reason for reading this book. There's some aspect of your memory that you want to improve because you think it will make you better in some way. Believe me, if you apply yourself to improving your memory, not only will you become better in whatever way you set out to when you picked up this book, but you will become better in nearly every facet of your life. Using the amazing resource that is your memory will make everything easier, faster, and better.

There are, of course, the practical aspects of an improved memory. Perhaps the most practical application is one that Paul Eckman, a psychologist, has developed for law enforcement agencies. Eckman has been cataloging facial expressions for seven years. Here's what he has found: "There are three hundred combinations of two facial muscles. If you add in a third, you get over three thousand. We took it up to five muscles, which is over ten thousand visible facial configurations." Those facial configurations — you and I would call them "expressions" — can't be manipulated. They truly show what is going on in a person's mind, how that person is feeling at a given moment. In seminars for law enforcement agencies Eckman teaches officers to identify which facial expressions represent dangerous intent on the part of a potential perpetrator and which can be considered harmless. These techniques undoubtedly have saved the lives of officers who otherwise wouldn't have recognized that they were in danger. At the same time, there is no doubt that the techniques have also saved the lives of innocent people who happened to be in the wrong place but whom the police recognized as not part of a dangerous situation.

I hope you won't have to use your memory to save your life. But you'll certainly find that you enjoy life more as your memory expands. Here are fourteen basic skills that I know are improved as a result of a better memory. Mastering your memory is mastering the thought process. The skills that you develop to improve your memory will also make you more efficient at work and more extraordinary at home.

1. *Observation.* As you understand and practice your memory development, you become keenly aware of how you receive information through your five senses.
2. *Perception.* Because your observation skills improve, you develop a heightened awareness of the world around you, increasing your ability to recognize and piece together clues.
3. *Analysis.* We were not designed to remember everything. Your mind naturally determines the relevancy, importance, and interest of incoming information.

Developing your memory improves your ability to compare, extract, correlate, evaluate, and differentiate.

4. *Interpretation.* A highly trained memory allows you to see and understand the world around you in enhanced ways that improve your ability to interpret what you see or hear and also your ability to make clear the meaning of something to someone else.

5. *Problem solving.* Some of the exercises in this book challenge your conventional way of thinking and remembering. You will learn to redirect and restructure your thought process in a way that leads to creative and innovative solutions.

6. *Systematizing.* You will be able to remember volumes of information you never thought possible, and organize information for easy retrieval. You develop mental methods to coordinate and develop procedures that make you as highly efficient as your thought process.

7. *Management.* Your brain is very efficient. Developing your memory teaches you how to mimic the brain's ability to manage information, resources, skills, abilities, and talents.

8. *Decision-making.* You understand why your memory retains what it does and you can extrapolate that ability to facilitate your selection process.

9. *Mentoring.* Improved memory increases your knowledge base, develops study and learning skills, and helps you become wiser. You are then able to help others grow personally and professionally.

10. *Innovation.* A well-developed memory devises and invents your strategies, which may at first seem strange. You are encouraged to truly "think outside the box" and break with convention.

11. *Imagination.* A well-developed memory is a developed imagination with an increased ability to visualize and conceptualize.

12. *Synthesis.* A highly trained memory can bring together ideas, tips, and other information that can be used to enrich your life.

13. *Listening.* You learn how to sift through the information you are hearing and capture its value through improved mental organization, focus, and concentration.

14. *Verbal presentations.* You develop mental organizational tools that allow

you to speak without having to refer to notes and to stay focused on the topic despite questions or sidebar conversations.

Now let's begin the process of shedding those preconceived notions that memory is a gift bestowed on someone else, not you, and learn to experience the full potential of the gift you didn't know you had.

Chapter Two
The "Write" Way
to Remember

Your natural memory defines who you are. It is the sum of the experiences and knowledge that you have accumulated up to this very moment in your life. It is your identity and relates everything about you. Without it, you are lost. It is a natural part of who you are. It is powerful. In an area about the size of your two clenched fists, you have millions of bits of information that can be assembled in a fraction of an instant when touched by a single thought.

Memory is like light. Unfocused, it is diffused and scattered. But a focused memory, much like the beam of a powerful laser, can cut through the barriers and limitations you may have inadvertently created in your mind about your memory. I know because for years I sabotaged my memory with such negative phrases as "I am always forgetting names" or that universal favorite, "Honey, have you seen my car keys?"

But a focused memory does far more than just burn away negativity. It enlightens and enriches your life by enhancing the way that you think. And how you think is directly tied to how you remember. The first step in your journey to that powerful, focused memory begins either on a piece of paper or on your computer screen. The best way to learn how you think and how you remember is to write down your experiences on a regular basis.

Creating Your Memory Baseline

One of my favorite authors is Stephen King. I love the imagination that goes into his compelling and scary stories and marvel at his immense output. In his book *On Writing*, King says that writing is really nothing more than refined thinking. And that's exactly what this exercise in journal keeping is — a way to refine your thinking. I'm not asking you to sit down in front of the computer for hours at a time crunching away at the Great American Novel that supposedly resides in all of us. But I am asking you to take a few moments at the end of each day to write down some of the things that happened. I'll also give you two simple tools that you can use to sharpen the focus of your memory. Too often we jot things down as a way of giving ourselves permission to forget. Once it's on the list, we don't have to remember it anymore (assuming we remember where we put the list). This kind of writing is different. This time you're writing down things because you want to remember them. Don't worry; you won't have to do this for the rest of your life to keep your memory sharp. It's just a way to help you understand what you naturally retain. Consider this a baseline exercise that a physical trainer might perform with a new client. The trainer's goal is to assess the client's strength before prescribing specific exercises to strengthen the body while taking into account weaknesses such as a bad knee.

The beauty of keeping a daily journal is that it reveals your natural strengths. You may be best at remembering names and faces or you may be very good at remembering numbers. By capturing various experiences on paper or on the computer screen, you can begin tapping in to the knowledge of the greatest expert on your memory — you. Together, we will use your journal to identify and develop four essential aspects of your memory.

The first aspect of your memory that the journal will help is your mental eye. When you sit down at the end of the day and write a bit about your experiences, you are mentally reconstructing the day. The first time you do this, some parts of the day will be startlingly clear. Others will be frighteningly hazy. But very quickly in this process you'll begin to remember more and more about each day. The goal isn't to remember everything. Rather, it's to become more aware each day of what is happening to you as it happens and of how you think about your various experiences.

The second aspect is identifying your interests. At the end of the day, your mind has filtered out a lot of information. The things you are recording are the things you have either consciously or unconsciously decided to keep for a while because you found them interesting, important, or both. The mind is like a miner panning for gold, sifting through the limitless volumes of water and debris, and keeping that which has potential value. Although we are capturing the value of the day by writing it down, we are also developing and analyzing the sifting process. While we like to think that we remember the things that are important to us, that isn't true. Haven't you had the experience of thinking, "I need to remember this because it's important," and then forgetting whatever it was five minutes later?

One of my best friends describes this phenomenon as "mental lint."

"I remember the most unimportant things," he marvels. "I can remember almost verbatim the superhero motto from the cartoon 'The Tick': *Evil comes in many forms. But whether it is a man-eating cow or Joseph Stalin you can't let the package hide the pudding. No sir. Because any way you slice it, evil is just plain bad. So you have to hit it across the nose with the rolled-up newspaper of goodness: 'bad dog.'*

"But," he continues, "I can't remember somebody's name ten seconds after I meet them."

Obviously, he is very good at remembering words and phrases: a left brain activity. There is also an element of humor in what he remembers. The Tick motto came from a television cartoon. He remembers that phrase after hearing it, not reading it, which suggests that his listening skills are well developed. There are ways that we'll explore later in the book to put such skills to even better use in developing our memories.

In the third aspect, you will identify which parts of your memory are already well developed, including input from your senses and emotions, both critical components of memory. By writings things down every day, at the end of the day, you will be able to identify the senses and emotions that you tend to use most frequently. That will enable you to play to those strengths, while making extra efforts to engage the senses and emotions that you don't use much now.

Finally, you will develop an understanding of the powerful nature of time's eraser. It's no secret that time decays some memories. In a classic study conducted by the German psychologist Hermann Ebbinghaus at the turn of the twentieth century, he concluded that we could forget 70 percent to 80 percent of studied material after only twenty-four to forty-eight hours have passed. These results can be extrapolated to your experiences during the day. How much do you remember from two days ago? Three? Four? We remember what we record. As you keep this journal for a few days, you will be amazed at the information you have captured that might otherwise have been lost in the whitewash of time. Perhaps you will find journal keeping such a useful exercise that you will continue it for a lifetime. Time works against you, but you can train your brain to mitigate its power by first recognizing its insidious nature and then practicing the techniques outlined in this book.

Recalling a Common Tragedy

As a simple exercise to demonstrate what you will be doing as you write your daily journal, let's share a common tragic moment in our past: September 11, 2001. Recall that day and try to remember as much as you can about where you were, what you were doing, and what emotions you felt when you learned about the attack on the World Trade Center towers and the Pentagon. I want you to write down as much detail as you remember. As a guide, here are my recollections:

On September 11, 2001, I was at a distribution warehouse in Dunn, North Carolina, evaluating the fire protection of their flammable liquid storage. The National Fire Protection Association codes are very strict about how hazardous liquids can and can't be stored under a closed roof and it's a time-consuming job to determine if the codes are being met. About mid-morning, I needed another shot of caffeine. I went to a break room and got a cup of black coffee from the vending machine. The thin paper cup offered scant insulation between the scalding liquid and my tender fingers, so I had to keep putting it down on one of several picnic tables that occupied at least half of the room. The maintenance supervisor, R. L. Moore, dressed in the blue denim jacket he always wore when we had to venture outside, asked me if I wanted to share a package of peanut butter crackers. Feeling hungry, I began to debate whether or not to get my own.

Just then, one of the truck drivers burst into the room and told us that he had heard on the radio that a plane had crashed into one of the towers in New York City. Accustomed to many practical jokes, I glanced around to see if anyone else shared my initial confusion and skepticism, but it was just the three of us. R.L. seemed surprised.

That was unusual. He had seen and heard just about everything in his sixty-plus years and he clearly thought the truck driver was sincere. I thought the driver's story was a little sketchy on details and I began to doubt what he was saying. I remember feeling confused, but not alarmed or frightened because I had no idea of the scope of the horrific events. It was only after we finally saw a television set about an hour later and watched the endless replays of the passenger jets slamming into the towers that the grief and sadness of the tragedy began to sink in.

I don't remember every detail about the event. For example, I don't remember the truck driver's name. I can't describe what he was wearing or repeat, word for word, what he said. But I am amazed at the detail of what I do remember, and this is what I want you to focus on — how much you remember, not how much you have forgotten. I suspect that your account of that horrible day will be somewhat similar to mine without employing any special memory techniques. Take a few moments now and write it down. Then we'll analyze some of the information.

Breaking Down Your Story

Review your story now to see if you can add some details. Do you remember the exact words from the source of the news? What did you do immediately after hearing the news of the attack? Do you remember any specific colors or shapes? Were there any specific smells or tastes that might have been part of the environment? Were you holding anything? How were you dressed? What sounds were there around you in the background?

Developing Your Focused Memory

Now that you have a narrative version of your 9/11 recollections, we're going to see which of your senses, emotions, and actions are part of that memory. As you learn to use your memory more effectively, you'll find that the beginning of each day isn't just a blank sheet of paper. Rather, you can think of it as one of those elaborately folded origami envelopes. As each event unfolds during the day, it is akin to unfolding one of those envelopes. Each of the folded sections of envelope can represent a variety of pictures, senses, feelings, and actions. After you've unfolded the envelope all the way, you can easily reconstruct its original structure by simply following the creases. Your natural memory works the same way. The starter questions merely give you the outline of the creases by which your natural memory reconstructs the day or events during the course of the day.

Our natural memory is an excellent and powerful tool. But we can rev up that tool significantly if we can focus our memory. A focused memory is also like an origami envelope but now it contains not just a recollection of things that happened, but information and knowledge that you have chosen specifically to remember because it will enrich your life. A focused memory is constructed the same way that a natural memory is reconstructed.

There are lots of ways to talk about focused memory, but I believe the simplest way to think about it is that focused memory results from an engaging experience. Each focused memory is carefully constructed using what I call Three Reversible Rules of Engagement:

1. A focused memory engages our Senses.

2. A focused memory engages our Emotions.
3. A focused memory engages our Actions.

When I think about my piano recital story, it includes several senses: the foreign feel of the piano keys, the shape of the baby grand piano, the voice of Mrs. Livesay as she spoke encouraging words, and, of course, the sound of silence. It also includes several emotions such as fear, stupidity, and a sense of impending doom. Distinct actions include walking toward the piano and then stumbling away from it. Those are the rules of engagement.

But why "reversible"? Simply because once we have laid down a specific memory involving our senses, emotions, and actions, a similar set of circumstances can take us back to that memory. When I was in the lead-lined room, the sound of the door being closed and the ensuing silence triggered the recital memory. Whenever I am on national television, there is pressure to perform because I am almost always being tested to remember a deck of playing cards and occasionally I feel myself begin to freeze up. When this happens, I am instantly reminded of being in front of the keyboard.

When you write to remember, you develop your mental eye by recording your senses, emotions, and actions throughout the day. Every event you have written down contains one or more of these components. If you like to use acrostics as a memory tool, you might want to remember the phrase "SEA to See" — our mental eye sees and records using our Senses, Emotions, and Actions.

When a memory is broken down this way, it appears to contain an infinite number of components and each of these components is essentially perfect. We never confuse sweet with bitter, silent with loud, aromatic with putrid, or angry with happy. We have an extraordinary ability to recognize thousands of odors, tastes, smells, textures, feelings, and movements.

An easy way to apply the Three Reversible Rules of Engagement is to set up a chart like the accompanying one, which I call an Element Box. The idea is to go down the chart putting checkmarks in the appropriate boxes. Does your 9/11 story, for instance, involve the tactile feel of anything, such as the hot coffee that burned my fingers? If so, put a checkmark under Yes across from Touch. If you were also holding your cat on your lap and recalled its soft fur, add another checkmark to Touch. If you were watching television news when you first learned about the attacks, you almost certainly would check Yes across from Sight and Sound. If you heard the news from a radio, you might check No for Sight but Yes for Sound. To avoid overwhelming the Sight category, count only specific shapes or colors. When you get down to Emotion, put a checkmark in the Yes box for each emotion you can identify. In my recounting I recorded at least four emotions: confusion, doubt, sadness, and grief. Thus I would have four checks in the Yes box for Emotion. Do the

The Element Box

Element	Yes	No
Touch		
Taste		
Sight		
Sound		
Smell		
Emotion		
Action		

same thing for Action. Did you call your spouse with the news? Did you turn on the television after a friend told you about the attacks? Those are both checks under Yes for Action.

Using Key Words

There's a final exercise related to your journal: the creation of key words. Go back to your narrative version of your 9/11 memories. Then, in a chart similar to the accompanying Key Word chart, summarize the individual events and experiences in your narrative into single words and put those "key words" in the left column. Leave the right column blank for now; it's there to help you tomorrow if you need it. Clearly the defining event of 9/11 was the destruction of the World Trade Center towers. Thus, I would simply write the word *towers* on the first line. That's one of my key words. But let's assume you met Anna at the grocery store that day and talked about the horrific events. You happened to notice that she was wearing a turquoise necklace. The two of you agreed to get together for lunch soon. I would distill that meeting with Anna down to the word *turquoise.* So my Key Word chart for 9/11 looks like this:

Key Word	Supplemental Element
Towers	
Turquoise	

Tomorrow morning I want you to come back to this Key Word chart and see if the words trigger explicit memories. *Towers* is a no-brainer: the collapse of the Trade Center towers and all the horror surrounding the event. But perhaps the word *turquoise* doesn't immediately trigger the grocery-store meeting with Anna, who was wearing a turquoise necklace. If you draw a blank, go back to your 9/11 narrative to find out what you meant by *turquoise.* It was the meeting with Anna, so write "Anna" under the heading Supplemental Element. So now your Key Word chart looks like this:

Key Word	Supplemental Element
Towers	
Turquoise	Anna

This is a fascinating exercise because it trains your brain to remember by using a bare minimum of resources. It is an efficient way to recall information because you are looking at one powerful visual word that triggers a plethora of memories. Your brain, over a surprisingly short period of time, develops the ability to capture the essence of the experience in a single word or vivid picture.

One of the main purposes of this exercise is to identify the strongest elements of your natural memory. For example, it isn't enough to know that you are a "visual" person. That's too broad. What you are interested in finding out is what specific parts of your visual memory are strong. Are you good at remembering shades of colors — navy, aqua, and turquoise — or just plain "blue"? Are you good at identifying specific facial expressions? Are you good at remembering the environment, and, if so, what specific objects about that environment can you recall? One of the reasons for identifying these elements is that if you remember something specific, then the general memory of the person, place, or thing renews itself. For example, the word *turquoise* may generate a memory of a necklace that you saw your friend Anna wearing when you ran into her at the grocery store. That memory, in turn, triggers a reminder that you promised to call her for lunch soon. It's like a camera that starts in close and then zooms out to fill in surrounding details.

Another reason to identify these strong elements is that you can use them to enhance what you want to remember. For instance, if you meet someone named Anna who looks nothing like the Anna you already know, you may notice that she is wearing a turquoise-colored top or blazer. This color is a trigger for your friend Anna with the turquoise necklace. You have now used a natural strength, color, to link or associate the new name with someone and something you already know.

Starting Your Journal

Make the commitment today to keep your journal. The sooner you begin, the faster you will develop your perfect memory. For the next week or so I'll ask you to develop your journal in three sections. First, of course, will be your written narrative of the day's events. You don't have to write down every single thing that happened to you — your shoelace broke when you were tying your shoes, for instance — only the things that have some significance. Just a word of caution, though: If you remember something like your shoelace breaking, don't immediately dismiss it as inconsequential. There might be a reason you remembered it that you simply haven't yet realized. The point is, the exercise should be fun and interesting. As soon as it stops being fun and interesting, you've written enough! To help you get started I've developed a wide-ranging list of starter questions. Don't try to answer them all. That would start to make the journal a tedious chore. Just pick a few that interest you. They'll help you see just how much you can remember within the framework of a day.

Observation

1. What did I see?
2. What did I hear?
3. What captured my attention?
4. Why was it interesting?
5. When did it happen during the day?

Events

1. What did I do today?
2. How is it relevant to the future or the past?
3. What am I gathering from my successes?
4. What do I want to learn from my failures?
5. What phone conversations did I have? What was said, not said, perceived?
6. What did I eat and drink today? What did I enjoy most or least?

People

1. Whom did I see?
2. What were they wearing?
3. What colors, what styles?
4. What were the conversations about? How long were they?
5. What did I learn about them? Myself? Was anything new? Was it repetitive?

6. How did I feel? Positive or negative or other? What's the source of the feeling?
7. What was the major content of the interaction? How does this affect me?
8. Did I meet anyone new? What were the names? Older, younger, my age?

Structure
1. How do I remember the order of the day?
2. Am I starting at the end, the middle, or the beginning?
3. Is it a mixture of all three?

Time
1. Where was my time spent today?
2. Was the majority spent on seeking treasures — achieving goals, celebrating successes, and creating value?
3. Was major time spent on minor things and activities?
4. Was I efficient today? Do I feel guilt or joy? Both?
5. Am I trying to suppress/forget some of the bad moments?

Environment
1. Am I remembering faces from today?

2. What was the environment like?
3. Am I remembering specific sounds? Tones in conversations? Music?
4. How much detail am I remembering? Can I see the stripes on the tie or suit?
5. Is the memory more of an overview, an impression, or a general feeling?
6. How much stress am I under, on a scale of 1 to 5?
7. What is the source of that stress?
8. How much sleep am I getting?

Developing Your Brain Skills

The list of starter questions may seem overwhelming, filled with both specific and general questions, but part of the purpose is to exercise your brain in different ways. In the late 1960s, Dr. Roger Sperry received the Nobel Prize for his research that revealed that the brain is divided into two halves and each half is responsible for a variety of skills. The right brain, for example, provides spatial awareness of three-dimensional shapes, giving us the ability to rotate objects in our mind. It also facilitates face recognition, visual imagery, music, imagination, color, and the ability to see the "whole picture." Artists, musicians, and other creative people tend to be right-brain dominant. The left side is a lot more disciplined. It handles logic, language, math, analytical abilities, sequences, patterns, and details. Engineers, scientists, and other technical people think of themselves as left-brain dominant. Simply visualizing what you have done during the day is a great right-brain activity. You are imagining the people you have met, you are seeing an overview of the day, and you are re-creating the experiences. Writing down what you see is a left-brain activity, as you form the words to analyze what you have seen, identify the structure of the day, and record some of the quantifiable knowledge that you have gathered. By writing down your experiences at the end of the day, you are exercising many of the same brain skills that are involved in creating and retrieving memories. Remember, you don't have to answer all the questions. Pick just a few that interest you.

After you've written the narrative part, construct the Element Box that I showed you earlier in this chapter. Although one of the purposes of the table is to help you record how you remember, its primary purpose is to make you aware of what elements you are using to remember. It shouldn't take more than a few minutes to put together the Element Box.

Finally, go back to the narrative you wrote and distill the main events into single key words as shown in the Key Word chart. Tomorrow morning, as you drink your coffee, review the previous entries by looking only at the key words. Within a week, I think you'll be amazed at the amount of information you have captured in just a few words. You are also fine-tuning the art of renewal. You are taking fragments of the day and re-creating the life of the experience. This will help you immensely when you are trying to recall the name of the person standing right in front of you. You can remember fragments about the person — i.e., where he works, how many syllables are in her name, etc. — but the actual name is very slow to develop. Practicing this exercise helps to develop your ability to breathe life into fragments.

I think these three exercises — writing a narrative of the day and constructing an Element Box and a Key Word chart — should be undertaken for several weeks, at least in part because we'll use them as the basis for learning how to build Roman

Rooms, perhaps the most valuable lesson in this book. I'm confident that after only the first week of keeping a journal, you'll discover an amazing power to reconstruct events and conversations that you never believed you could. Once you realize the power of this simple approach to an improved memory, I think you'll want to continue it, perhaps not every day, but often enough to keep in practice.

Chapter Three

Making Sense of Our Senses

There's a tendency in many human beings to be skeptical. Often we don't believe something can be done until we've done it ourselves. Take flying in an airplane, for instance. Intellectually we know planes can fly. We've seen and heard them passing overhead many times. But sight and hearing are just two of our senses. You may be one of those people who need to experience more. Only after you've belted yourself into a seat as the engines begin to rev up, felt the jouncing movement and tremendous acceleration as the aircraft rumbles down the runway, and experienced the sensation of lifting off the ground and into the air are you totally convinced that this thing can fly. You've used almost all your senses to experience the act of flying. So it is with memory. You will begin to feel the inherent power of your memory after you have kept your journal for a few days. In this chapter we're going to explore more deeply how to use all your senses to supply vital input for creating memories.

Glowing and Growing

Recall what Dr. Paul Laurienti of Wake Forest University Medical Center told us earlier about what happens when we either see or hear a fire engine compared to both seeing and hearing it. When our senses of sight and sound are engaged, our brain responds much more powerfully than it does when only one of these senses is active. Research shows that as more and more senses are activated, there is an ever-increasing activation in our brain that subsequently increases our natural ability to remember. You now know, as the result of keeping your journal, that it would be a dull day indeed if we didn't use more than two of our senses. The full engagement of all our senses, and the resulting growth in our ability to remember and process information, is perhaps most obvious in how clearly we remember some events, such as a particularly fine day at the beach, our first date, a wedding, or, sadly, a family funeral. All are events that involve almost all of our senses and emotions. It's a phenomenon that I call "Glow and Grow." The more elements we can make glow in our brain, the more our memories can grow.

When you are keeping your journal you're not invoking any special memory techniques. You're simply glowing and growing.

Creating Mental Icons

In the preceding chapter, we discussed how writing things down at the end of the day helps to develop your mental eye. The questions and key words used in the lists and tables probably brought to mind a picture at first, after which you added additional details. I call the first picture that came to mind a mental icon — your brain's equivalent of the little symbols on your computer screen — and as we work to improve our memory we will use more and more mental icons. This exercise will show you how to construct an icon from scratch rather than just take whatever impressions are already in your mind to build a picture.

Let's start by creating icons for the elements of a simple list. I've found that there are five basic questions you can ask any person to get to know much more about him or her.

1. Do you have any children?

2. Where do you live?
3. What kind of work do you do?
4. Where do you like to travel?
5. What are your favorite sports or hobbies?

Since these five questions are such effective tools in getting to know someone, they're worth remembering. Rather than just stare at the questions, repeating them numerous times to try to imprint them on your mind, let's instead build a mental icon that represents all five questions. The first two questions — "Do you have any children?" and "Where do you live?" — could be depicted in our mind's eye as two young children entering a log cabin in the woods. The third question — "What kind of work do you do?" — might be represented as a leather work glove serving as the chimney for the little log cabin. We might even see smoke coming out the ends of the glove fingers. "Where do you like to travel?" can be represented by an airplane being held in the glove. And the last question — "What are your favorite sports and hobbies?" — can be symbolized by a tennis racket on the side of the plane where we ordinarily see the airline's logo.

Doubtless your mental image of what

we've just constructed would contain different details from mine. But the major elements, the distinct images that let us remember the five basic questions, are present in all of our minds' eyes: the children, the cabin, the work glove, the airplane, and the tennis racket. Each of these five images represents one of the fundamental questions, but each image is also blended together into one painting in your mind. The individual components construct the overall picture so that a single portrait represents the entire thing we want to remember. This is a beautiful example of synergy and how the brain works to become efficient. By blending individual elements the brain creates an icon, a symbol for a vast amount of information and knowledge.

Once you have an icon in your mind, you need to imprint it deeply so that it will withstand the eraser of time. To do that, you need to employ more of your senses. You want the icon to "glow and grow." So let's add some sensory flesh to our picture by hearing the children laugh as they run toward the little cabin. Then rub your hand over the exterior of the cabin, feeling the rough texture of the logs. You might conjure up the combined smell of leather and smoke to add sensory inputs to the image of the work glove. The jet's engines, of course, are making lots of noise and producing the distinctive odor of burned jet fuel. Finally, you can feel and hear the *thwock* of a solidly hit tennis ball.

Now what was merely a list of five questions has become something much more rich and enduring: an experience that comes to life through the sensory elements you applied.

Your Picture Perfect Memory

The creation of that mental icon to help you remember five basic questions illustrates a fundamental quality of memory: your memory is virtually picture perfect. You had no trouble seeing in your mind's eye the five important elements of the icon: children, a cabin, a glove, a plane, and a tennis racket. In fact, research suggests that we never lose the ability to recognize or remember what we have seen, unless we have a disease like Alzheimer's or another form of dementia, and even then parts of our long-term memory remain intact.

Okay, so you're a little skeptical of the statement I just made. You can think of incidents in which you've forgotten things. There are the names of those people you met at the party last week, the e-mails you were going to answer, maybe even the date of your anniversary. That's fine. If you could remember every last thing you saw and did, you would have a photographic memory and that would be a terrible thing.

What, you thought this book was all about developing a photographic memory? Sure, the cover promises to reveal the mind's extraordinary power to remember things. But there's a vast and important difference between a photographic memory and a powerful memory, and that difference is the power of choice.

Consider the digital camera, a true marvel of technology. At the touch of a button the camera can capture the extremes of incredible beauty and abject horrors in all their minute details. But for all of its wonders, it is a mindless miracle. It will record a chest full of the king's treasures and a bag full of garbage with the same exacting detail. It can't distinguish between what is worth recording and what is a waste to record. Wouldn't it be terrible to have a truly photographic mind, recording everything that you see, hear, and experience with the same detail as a camera lens? Although a large part of this book is dedicated to refining and improving your memory, we need to keep in mind that forgetting is just as much of a blessing because there are things in our lives that we simply don't want or need to remember.

Developing Pictures in Your Mind

At the next party you attend, watch the eyes of people when they are being introduced to someone. You'll likely see their eyes move up and down, literally measuring the person they're meeting. That's a good example of how the brain thinks and remembers.

Try this exercise. Sit in a room and think about what your eyes are seeing. Notice how your focus flits from one spot to the next. As you do this, you become aware of the amazing amount of detail that your eyes are taking in. The room has depth, color, and shape and contains a number of objects, each with its unique characteristics. Our minds naturally construct detailed pictures of the environment around us. Perhaps it is one of those primal instincts that we were born with, because back in our

Neanderthal days the nature of our environment was fundamental to survival.

Ken Burns's excellent documentaries, many of which are aired on PBS, are memorable because he is constantly doing something with the camera. Although he uses old photographs, drawings, and paintings of historic events, he doesn't focus just on the picture itself, he moves the camera, panning in and out and across the painting as a kind of vicarious physical eye. The effect is to help the viewer re-create the environment of a history long past. His method is so engaging that we may actually feel as if we are there, experiencing the sight of buffalo as far as the eye can see or of the battle of Custer's last stand. History is not my favorite subject, unless Ken Burns is the teacher.

This ability of the mind to create and remember an environment by developing pictures of what we have seen and where we have been is critical to understanding how we begin to organize the information that we want to remember. What's nice is that it's easy to do because we already think in pictures, although you might not realize that. What do you see in your mind's eye when I ask, "What did you have for breakfast today?" Perhaps you instantly see the bowl of cereal, or the bagel, or the scrambled eggs on the plate. If you think about it — we usually don't — the mental picture you've just drawn will contain a surprising amount of detail, including colors and textures. The glistening yellow eggs sit on a white plate that in turn is on a brown wooden table, all of which is on a light blue tile floor surrounded by patterned wallpaper leading up to an off-white ceiling. The visual nature of our memories automatically includes the shapes of the plate, the bowl, the table, and even distinguishes the wallpaper pattern. But also note that every object is linked to its environment. It's not just eggs suspended in a void of nothingness; the eggs are on the plate that's on the table, and so on. It's all about connectivity. The picture in your mind's eye literally reflects the way your brain thinks. One item is connected to another that is connected to another and so on for infinity. Your mind is always developing pictures.

Developing Your Picture Memory

The secret to developing your virtually perfect memory is to use what is already perfect within you. We think in terms of pictures. Pictures are perfect. We remember in terms of experiences that are constructed with hundreds and even thousands of perfect elements we categorize as senses, emotions, and actions. Remember the phrase "SEA to See"? That's the code for my Three Reversible Rules of Engagement. Memory engages the Senses, the Emotions, and Action. When we convert words and phrases into pictures and experiences, we unlock the unlimited potential of our memory.

In order to practice using the rules of engagement, let's use another list of things we might want to remember. In Rick Warren's best-seller, *The Purpose Driven Life*, he discusses the five most common things that drive our lives: guilt, anger, fear, materialism, and approval. We could memorize that list by rote or we could use the Three Reversible Rules of Engagement to create engaging experiences. Although it is always better to use your own experiences, here are the ways in which I approached this exercise.

I equate "fear" with the only time I ever entered a golf competition. I was in my late twenties and it was nothing but a longest-drive contest. The problem was that many more competitors and spectators turned out for the event than I had expected. I never really appreciated the pressure that huge crowds must put on professional golfers until I heard my name called. I was so nervous, I couldn't get my legs to stop shaking. Driving a golf ball a long way is an art form of balance and strength. A great swing looks effortless because it is all about perfect timing and focused power. Apparently, when it comes to onlookers, even my muscle memory fails me, because my whole body seemed to be trembling. There was no good reason for it, and I couldn't stop it. As the crowd maintained a respectful silence, my biggest fear was that I would miss the ball because the club was shaking, too. I hit the ball, barely. It went straight up in the air. If there had been a good wind blowing in my face, I feel certain that ball would have gone backward. Thus, I equate fear with shaking.

"Guilt" is easy for me. I just envision the sound of my neighbor's lawn mower as I'm sneaking out to the car to drive to the golf course.

I can generate an image of "anger" by looking at my scorecard from that guilty round of golf. I scored a lousy 106 strokes, lost two golf balls, and threw a new putter that didn't work well into the water trap. How's that for anger?

I've always thought of fancy cars, specifically the Mercedes-Benz line, as the ultimate expression of "materialism." So that's what I envision driving to the golf course.

Finally, "approval" is the smile on my wife's face when she realizes I really did get three things on the to-do list done that morning before heading out to play golf.

Now all I have to do is distill these mental experiences into single concepts. For me, they would be:

Fear — shaking
Guilt — lawn mower
Anger — scorecard
Materialism — Mercedes
Approval — smile

Finally, I create a simple visual story: I see my wife smiling as I am riding on my Mercedes lawn mower. I mow right over my golf scorecard and the lawn mower shakes as it rips that card to shreds.

Developing your picture memory is more than just creating a series of images, because your natural memories are more than just two-dimensional pictures. They are multidimensional experiences equipped with emotions and actions that give the memory depth, interest, and meaning.

Action is another important component of memory. Imagine sitting in a conference or a classroom with all eyes focused on the facilitator. Suddenly, someone arrives late and makes his way from the back to find an open seat. What will every head in the room do? Turn. For that seemingly insignificant moment, the movement captures our attention. It is an unconscious reaction because our eyes are trained for movement. If our physical eye is trained for movement, then so is our mental eye. Yet, when we hear the term *visualize,* we tend to see static pictures, not necessarily the movement within them.

Returning to Rick Warren's list of motivational factors and focusing on the word *approval,* I immediately think of my father. Perhaps his image springs to mind because children have a fundamental need for parental favor. But because my father also represents so many other things in my life, it is important to narrow that image to this one category, "approval." I know, from life experience, that whenever he is pleased with something, my father nods his head a certain way.

Searching for a Photographic Memory

Is there even such a thing as a photographic memory? Dr. K. Anders Ericsson, Conradi Eminent Scholar and Professor of Psychology at Florida State University, has been looking for the answer to this question for over twenty years, studying people with extraordinary, seemingly photographic, recall.

The answer to this question probably came to light in an interview he gave The Discovery Channel in May 2001. The segment featured one of his research subjects, a man known simply as Rajan, a young graduate student with extraordinary recall for numbers. Rajan can recite the value of pi (3.141519 . . .) to several thousand places and is capable of remembering fifty random digits with perfect accuracy after only about a minute of study. To prove that he had this extraordinary recall, Dr. Ericsson wrote a series of random numbers on a chalkboard that looked something like this:

```
1 2 3 7 0
1 4 1 5 9
2 7 3 9 4
1 3 2 5 8
0 2 9 4 7
```

After about a minute and a half of study, Rajan closed his eyes and quickly recalled every number. When asked, he recited the numbers backward. It appeared that, like a high-resolution scanner, Rajan was creating a perfect image of the number grid in his mind's eye and simply reciting what he was seeing on his mental screen. The obvious conclusion: Rajan has a photographic memory.

Or does he?

Dr. Ericsson then asked Rajan to go through the list of numbers naming only those single digits that occurred in a diagonal pattern. He would be expected to name the large boldface digits in the sequence we just saw above:

```
1 2 3 7 0
1 4 1 5 9
2 7 3 9 4
1 3 2 5 8
0 2 9 4 7
```

There was a long pause. Rajan's face showed signs of struggle. As he began naming numbers, his recitation took on a staccato, hesitating manner. Although he recited the designated numbers in the proper order, it took him about a minute to accomplish what should have been a simple task for someone with an essentially photographic memory. His interrupted recall of the numbers provided important evidence that his memory isn't photographic. Certainly he was not seeing a mental picture of the numbers on the chalkboard. If he were, he would have been able to see the grid in his mind and effortlessly repeat the diagonal numbers.

Dr. Ericsson explained that Rajan's extraordinary recall of numbers was the result of a system that he created and had been using all his life, a perplexing combination of stories and personal events that he associated with each number or series of numbers. For example, the first four numbers were somehow associated with his alarm clock. The next three numbers were linked to a cab he had taken to get to the show. He was using recent events of his day and associating them with the random numbers on the board.

Dr. Ericsson's conclusion: No one has a photographic memory. We can all take encouragement from that. It means that great memory feats are possible and that the ability to do these can be developed by anyone.

We unconsciously sense another person's level of engagement in conversation with us through nonverbal clues. Body language, subtle movements, and facial expressions give us tremendous accuracy in what that person is feeling or thinking. If we are trying to persuade someone and we see negative clues such as anger or boredom, we recognize these immediately and change our tactics.

Successful poker players are experts at picking up on what they call "tells." In the movie *Maverick*, the character played by Jodie Foster was ousted from the big tournament because every time she had a good hand she held her breath, twisted her hair, or drummed her fingers on her teeth.

Sign language can be a very effective method not only to learn text but to distill ideas down into a single movement. My wife, Janet, is a kindergarten teacher and some years she has as many as twenty-five five-year-olds in her classroom. By teaching them basic sign-language movements for "yes," "no," "good," "sorry," "happy," "quiet," and "sit," she is able to communicate to a child far across the room with a single motion while still giving attention to the child in her immediate vicinity. Depending on the sign, the child remembers the rewards or consequences indicated by the motion.

A focused memory lies in the conversion of words and ideas into pictures and experiences by using the Three Reversible Rules of Engagement. In chapter 4, we will expand your memory by blending associations and creating interests.

Chapter Four
Association and Interest

Remember the problem I had trying to use mnemonics to recall the organization of living things and the order in which the planets orbit the sun? I used the sentence King Philip Came Over For Good Spaghetti (Kingdom, Phylum, Class, Order, Family, Genus, and Species) for the order of life, and My Very Educated Mother Just Served Us Nine Pizzas (Mercury, Venus, Earth, Mars, Jupiter, Saturn, Uranus, Neptune, and Pluto) for the planets. Then, on the big test, I couldn't remember whether my mother served us pizza or spaghetti.

I'm certainly not alone in my inability to use tricks like this effectively. One of my friends complained recently about all the improve-your-memory articles that use the principle of association to help boost memory skills. "The problem is that the articles refer to crazy associations that don't make sense to me," he said. "One article showed me a face and gave her name as Mrs. Friar. The writer suggested I envision a medieval friar, complete with his brown robe, sitting on top of her head. On the next page, when I saw her face without the name, all I could think of was "monk." So I wrote, "Mrs. Monk."

I've always felt a bit negative about the word *association* when it comes to memory improvement. It gives the impression that the road to mental greatness is nothing more than a path paved with bizarre memory tricks. I saw the legendary mnemonics expert Harry Lorayne on the Johnny Carson show years ago. He memorized the names of everyone in the audience, an impressive mental feat. When asked how he did it, he said he associated every name with something bizarre. As an example, he pointed to a couple, Mr. and Mrs. Bird, and said he remembered their name by seeing two yellow canaries in a cage sitting on their foreheads. Clearly, the method worked well for him. But it held no interest for me. It seemed too difficult, with too much additional information to remember. Canaries, cages, and other bizarre imagery interfered with the name because they overloaded my short-term memory. Besides, they called for creativity and imagination, two skills I lack.

I did a lot of reading while recovering

from cancer, and I recall a quote in the book *Words I Wish I Wrote*, by Robert Fulghum. In a section titled "Companions" he collected this thought by Sir James G. Frazer: ". . . things which have once been in contact with each other continue to act on each other at a distance after the physical contact has been severed."

I could see how the quote pertained to companions, friends, and other relationships. I'd had childhood friends who kept me out of trouble and teenage friends who got me into trouble. I remember mentors I had in school and at work whose advice, guidance, and good counsel still influence me even though I have not seen them for twenty or thirty years.

But this phrase seemed to contain something more. The words stayed with me like a song I couldn't get out of my head. I churned them around in my mind until, a few days later, I modified the idea with something I call the Law of Association. It occurred to me that if this principle was about influence, then why should the influence be limited to personal relationships? Couldn't any two thoughts be automatically associated? In other words, wasn't it possible to connect any two ideas, pictures, or objects? Could I use my natural surroundings as visual reminders of what I wanted to remember?

The Law of Association

My wife, Janet, turns on a light in our laundry room every time she puts a load of clothes in the washer. That way, she doesn't forget that there are wet clothes, which could sour if left too long. Janet uses a physical reminder. I wanted to use my mind and imagination to create a similar reminder. For example, suppose I wanted to remember the names of the seven dwarfs. Could I imagine them in our home, and, if so, what kinds of things might they be doing? I could see Grumpy pouring a cup of coffee, Sneezy sniffing the pepper in the pantry, Doc rumbling around in the medicine cabinet, Bashful hiding in a closet, Dopey standing with one foot in the mop bucket, Sleepy on the sofa, and Happy sipping a glass of wine. Using the SEA to See method, the vision or experience in my mind became just as real as if we had friends visiting who had done the same kinds of things. All I was doing was remembering what had happened.

Denis Waitley, in his successful book and tapes from years ago, *The Psychology of Winning*, discusses brainwashing techniques. He believes that the mind cannot distinguish between what is real and what is vividly imagined. To make the point, he cites the case of the American prisoner during the Vietnam War who mentally played a round of golf every day during his years of captivity. When he finally returned to the United States, he shot par on his first round of golf. How in the world could he do that? Simple, he said, he had never made an errant shot in his mind during all those years.

So now when I look at the pot of coffee brewing in the kitchen, I am reminded of Grumpy even though he is not there. His physical contact with the coffeepot continues to act on it by reminding me of who poured it. If I could remember something as silly as the seven dwarfs in this manner, could I not associate any two things?

The answer, of course, is yes.

The power of the Law of Association allows you to create reminders within reminders, using your physical environment to link those memories to real objects. You naturally associate many things with your immediate environment. When our only daughter, Kristen, went off to college, the first few weeks were very difficult because there were reminders of her everywhere. The sight of her clean room and made-up bed was heartbreaking because I knew she was no longer at home. The ceiling downstairs, which had once resonated with the sound of her dancing feet as she listened to music in her bedroom, was now silent. The milk jug in the refrigerator stayed full.

The Law of Association is powerful because we use it every day. Learning to focus that natural power increases our knowledge, enhances learning, and makes us smarter because we can remember more things, allowing us to make better decisions and to ask better questions.

In a radio interview I conducted with Richard Israel, coauthor of *Brain Sell*, he gave an excellent example of the law.

Richard said, "Scott, I'm going to throw out two completely different words here, and I want you to see if you can link them together with a single image or idea. The words are *elephant* and *banana*."

These are contrasting images — a large gray mammal and a relatively small yellow fruit. Yet, in my mind, I could see the elephant wrapping his trunk around the banana to pull it from the tree — even though, to my knowledge, elephants don't eat bananas.

This single picture, a blend of two images, is the result of an instant and automatic association. To my surprise, the logical part of my brain enhanced the image instead of trying to dissolve it because I didn't know if elephants ate bananas — a mildly bizarre thought.

Sometimes, because something is a little bit unusual, that is enough to make it memorable. The brain, to fight boredom, requires constant stimulation, and something that stands out captures the brain's attention. Psychologists refer to this phenomenon as the Von Restorff effect. For example, in this list, it is pretty easy to determine which item is different: chair, deck, tree, bottle, Sean Connery, fence, post, and grass.

The phenomenon is useful when I am trying to remember a long list of ordinary names. For example, one of the most eloquent names I've come across is Tomorrow Hughes; it's unusual and almost poetic. Therefore, it stands out and I recall the young lady.

But bizarre works only if everything around it is ordinary. If everything around it is equally bizarre, the Von Restorff effect no longer applies.

In the 2003 World Memory Championships, held in Kuala Lumpur, Malaysia, an event required contestants to remember up to ninety-nine names and faces after fifteen minutes' study time. I do very well in this event in the U.S. competitions because I know lots of common names — Bob, Sara, Steve, Barbara, etc. However, because there is such an international contingent representing countries all over the world, almost all the names and faces presented during the event were strange and bizarre to me. I became overwhelmed when none of the names stood out.

Every time you learn and remember something, physical changes take place in your brain that make memory more efficient. As long as we focus on mental activities and give ourselves mentally challenging tasks, our brain cells continue to grow and expand, making a virtually unlimited number of connections and patterns.

A thought is real. It aligns brain cells, it creates patterns, and it causes chemicals to be released in our brains. Association is not a trick; it is how we are made to think.

Practicing and Applying
the Law of Association

The brain is logical. It uses associations and patterns to predict what will happen next. Turn this page upside down and try to read the passage in large boldface type. Be aware of what is happening.

YOUR BRAIN CHANGES FROM ITS ABILITY TO READ FROM LEFT TO RIGHT TO RIGHT TO LEFT. IN THE BEGINNING YOU FIND THAT YOU ARE READING EVERY LETTER IN THE FIRST FEW WORDS. BUT SOON, YOUR BRAIN WILL BEGIN TO ASSOCIATE THE FIRST FEW LETTERS AND THEN TO PICK UP THE PATTERN TO PREDICT WHAT THE NEXT WORD WILL BE.

Your brain will look for a verb after a noun and you will find that you are predicting the meaning of the sentence before you finish reading it.

There are benefits to this exercise. First, there is a dramatic improvement in your focus as your brain figures out what is happening. Second, you are amazed when you are able to make sense out of apparent nonsense. Third, you expand your retention skills to hold the information longer in your head because it takes you longer to read the sentence.

The exercise demonstrates how association is an inherent ability. It is an involuntary response like breathing or the beating of your heart. Just as physical exercise improves your heart rate, mental exercise increases your efficiency of association. It is important to fine-tune this ability because you are developing and strengthening the perfect nature of your memory.

Exercise 1

Perform the exercise that Richard Israel gave to me by flipping through this book and choosing two words at random. Don't confine yourself to nouns and verbs. Throw in a few prepositions, adjectives, and conjunctions to spice things up. Then construct a sentence. For example, the two words that I picked are *logical* and *embedded.* My sentence is: It is logical that associations are embedded in the way we think.

Try this exercise a couple of times and you will be amazed at your ability to associate any two random words.

Exercise 2

Next, look at the sentences you constructed with the two words you picked out. Now, take those two words and make a picture in your mind of each of them. Depending on the words you picked out, it might be very easy or you may encounter some mental resistance. Resistance is a good thing. It helps us mark out our perceived limits, only to find, when we have pushed past them, that we are better and stronger and more capable than we realized. Remember, memory is like a muscle. Without resistance, we cannot build strength, nor can our minds grow.

It is here, probably more than in any other exercise, that people want to give up because it seems too hard. And it is here, more than in any part of this book, that I truly feel your pain. In the National Memory Championships, held in New York City every year since 1998, one of the events I dread is the poem-memorization competition. In this event, contestants are given an unpublished poem that does not rhyme and are required to memorize as much of it as possible — verbatim. After fifteen minutes of study, the contestants are asked to write the poem, exactly as they saw it, word for word (spelled correctly), punctuation for punctuation, capital for capital, and so on.

Scoring for the event is as cruel as the memorization is grueling. Every line with more than one mistake, whether it is a misspelling, an incorrect word, a forgotten word, a misplaced comma, or improper spacing between lines, is counted as wrong. This is an extraordinarily difficult event for me, and one that always has the outcome of the entire competition hanging in the balance.

Over years of practicing for this formidable event, I have learned some very vital lessons about visualization. As you practice visualization, for example, you will probably find, as I did, that imagery of concrete words comes instantly but imagery of abstract words takes much longer because you have to devise symbols. For example, visualize the word *brick,* then visualize the word *freedom.* Brick is easy, freedom not so easy. And think about visualizing *and* or *but.*

I always use the first image that comes to mind. For the word *and* I immediately see an ampersand. For the word *but,* I see, well, a butt. I hope you have come to understand and appreciate that the brain recalls at lightning speed without giving us time to "think" about anything. The comprehension of letters and words on this page is proof of this. For me, the word *logical* brings to mind Mr. Spock of *Star Trek* fame, complete with raised eyebrow and the Vulcan salute, a raised hand, palm outward, with a **V**-split between the middle and the ring finger. Sometimes we may not know why an image comes to mind, but it doesn't matter; it just happens.

Don't let yourself be distracted about why something comes to mind. The mind consists of two very powerful but opposite forces — the power to focus and the desire to drift. Although it may be interesting to find out why a particular image comes to mind, such rabbit chasing will invariably distract us from our task. Since one of the primary goals of this book is to focus your memory, we need to do just that: stay focused.

Use at least one of the Three Reversible Rules of Engagement to transform the two-dimensional picture in your mind into a multi-dimensional experience: SEA to see. I may hear the baritone voice of Leonard Nimoy say, "Live long and prosper," or I might just see the movement of his hand as he makes the Vulcan salute.

But what about the second word we are visualizing, *embedded?* The term has become familiar to many people because it describes the U.S. military policy of allowing reporters to accompany military units in the conflict in Iraq. A reporter assigned to a military unit is said to be "embedded" in the unit. Using the Law of Association, which allows us to make connections between any two words, however unrelated they may be, I blend the two concepts. I see Mr. Spock not on the *Starship Enterprise* but as a correspondent on CNN reporting on the war. This whole process occurred in a second or two, but it took about a hundred times as long to write it down.

At this point, I hope you are intrigued and excited about the unlimited possibilities that the ability to associate has for your life. Pictures and experiences remain relatively perfect in our minds long after words have faded away. Pictures not only give us the ability to transform powerful ethereal ideas into tangible forms, but they are easily stored in our long-term memory. It is a way of manipulating infinity. An infinite amount of information stored in a finite reservoir that we call our mind.

However, I also realize that you may be equally resistant and want to resign from this exercise, perhaps finding the whole thing moderately amusing but not really practical in the everyday world. If you are entertaining this thought, let me ask you to entertain this one as well: Great resistance often marks the spot where great rewards can be found.

Up to this point you have been using association and visualization unconsciously every day, just as you use the light of the sun to get around. You convert the word *breakfast* to a mental picture of eggs. You convert the phrase *What did you do on your vacation?* to images of Disney World or maybe the gambling tables in Las Vegas. The point is, you've been doing this all along. Now, you're going to start doing it consciously.

There are three benefits to the Law of Association and the art of visualization. First, you will increase your intellectual capital by developing your imagination and expanding your creativity. These two assets are the currency of the future. Is it just coincidence that General Electric, one of the most recognized companies in the world, changed its long-standing motto "We bring good things to life" to "Imagination at work"? Imagination has driven the incredible expansion of technology, giving us tools that few of us would have dreamed of only a decade ago.

Using association and visualization will also give your mind a focal point on which to dwell. It is difficult, if not impossible, to focus on vague or abstract concepts. We need a tangible image or symbol to represent an idea. These techniques will also increase the speed at which you learn. By associating a new thought or idea with information that already exists in our long-term memory, we can instantly integrate the new concept into our thinking process. We are momentarily, if not permanently, changed in some way as the result of this new association. We'll explore these benefits in later chapters. But before we go into those details, there are some additional concepts you should be thinking about.

Interest

Of all the natural methods that we use to remember something, interest, by far, is the easiest and simplest. Simply put, we remember what interests us. And what interests us isn't necessarily what is important to us. Take television and movies. Most television programs and movies are not life-altering events. Yet, we remember scenes from our favorite movies and programs because they were entertaining. They *engaged* us. They *interested* us.

If you've seen the movie *Planet of the Apes*, starring Charlton Heston, I think you'll agree that there isn't anything important about it. Yet, I will stay up until the wee hours watching a rerun and waiting for my favorite line: "Get your stinking paws off me, you damn dirty ape."

I love it! That warning sends a shock through the mass of monkeys as they suddenly begin to doubt their superiority to a mere human being. If I try to put the best gloss on my love of that scene, I might think that it is a reflection of some deeper interests of mine. Perhaps my feelings about that scene reflect my concern about social injustice, racial prejudice, conformity, and the travesty of trying to suppress the differences in others. Maybe I'm sensitive to related issues such as cruelty, the establishment, fear of change, and blind obedience.

Sometimes we don't really know what we are interested in until we write it down. This is another reason why it is so important to write to remember. It helps you define and analyze your interests. A salesman once told me after one of my lectures that he used to think he had a terrible memory for names and faces. Then he realized that his business was not about the product he was selling. Rather, it was all about establishing relationships. His interest in people became paramount to success, and now he has a remarkable ability to remember names.

Some people are very good at remembering details such as batting averages, shooting percentages, or a plethora of other statistics that sports seem to generate. For people with such interests, sporting events become as much an exercise in calculating probabilities as they are a competition.

Take a few minutes to make a list of some of your passions. Then break each passion down to its indivisible core. For example, you may have a passion for cooking, which is a combination of art and science. You may like to start at the very beginning and follow the step-by-step instructions of a recipe. You combine specific ingredients in precise measurements with other ingredients. This is followed by a particular sequence of operations, including stirring, folding, blending, baking, etc. Sometimes you can substitute ingredients to enhance the taste or the visual nature of the dish. Cooking is a blend of combining details to create an overall effect.

Perhaps you have a passion for playing golf. A friend asks you how you did at the end of the round. You say, "I shot a 95." That statement is a simple fact. But there's a story behind it.

Since your average round of golf is about 80, you begin to explain. "On the very first hole, which you know has a severe dogleg to the left, I sliced my drive out-of-bounds. My fourth shot went to the very back of the green, but the hole position was up front on the very bottom end of that sloping tier. I three-putted and that was just the beginning of a very bad day." Now that you've added lots of supporting details, the story of that lousy round of golf is developing nicely.

Passions and interests, broken down in this way, give clues to how you construct a memory. Perhaps you start at the beginning by layering a sense of touch to a mental picture to create an experience. Or perhaps you start with an experience and then break it down to reveal the specific details that make the memory relevant.

Next, apply the Law of Association to the interests you have defined and see what imaginative and creative opportunities you can develop. Interest is like the canvas on which the picture is painted. Defining our interests provides the background to help us build our memories and gives us a way to remember whatever we want to. Let's say you want to remember a short grocery list. You know that you're one of those people who start at the very beginning and proceed in a step-by-step fashion to their goal. Make each item on the list part of a mental recipe that you are concocting to make an exotic dish. To keep the logical part of your brain from dissolving the mental recipe due to the combination of items that seem not to make sense, simply ask yourself this question: "How would that taste?" This simple thought allows both sides of your brain to work together. The right side of your mind is the mental eye, where you see the tangible pictures of the list, and the left side contains the analytical skill that determines why the images are there.

The point is, your memory engages with the things about which you're passionate. Therefore, you know you have a good memory. All you have to do now is apply it to things about which you may not be so passionate but which can be useful or entertaining. That's what we'll do in the next few chapters.

Chapter Five
The Art and Science
of Repetition

You've heard the old saying about the three most important things in selecting real estate: location, location, location. Unfortunately, too many people assign a similar importance to a basic memory technique: repetition, repetition, repetition. They seem to think that if we just hammer away hard enough and long enough with brute repetitive force, we'll chisel the information into our long-term memory.

How sad.

When we approach memory through brute repetition, we become slaves to it. We think that if we "just do the time" we will eventually earn freedom from the monotony. It doesn't take long, though, before we begin to ask ourselves, "How much is enough?" That quickly evolves into, "When can I stop?" What is most discouraging is that memorizing through repetition is too often the way we or our children are taught to learn in school. I don't know about you, but if I never hear the voice of "Multiplication Mallory" intoning again and again that "three times three is nine," it will be too soon. How many valuable hours are wasted the night before exams as students across the country cram in order to recall names, dates, and definitions?

Clearly, we give repetition too much weight in the memory process. Just consider how many things you see or hear only once and yet can recall without trying and without error? I can remember my first date with Janet, the first time I drove a car, my first (and only!) hole-in-one, and my first day on my first job. These memories come to me easily despite the fact that each was a onetime event.

A teacher in our local school system introduces sign language to several groups of first-graders. Each group is shown how to sign the alphabet once. Each letter is pronounced at the same time as the specific hand position for that letter is shown. The children immediately repeat the letter back. At the end of the exercise, the teacher spells out words and sentences by sign language and the children write down what they see. You'll probably be amazed to learn that over 90 percent of the children get every letter, word, or sentence, a true testament to the ability to memorize without repetition.

But the results aren't so amazing if you recall Dr. Paul Laurienti's comments about the fire engine and how both seeing and hearing it engages two parts of the brain, as opposed to the single parts that are engaged if we only hear or only see the fire engine. Sight combined with sound creates brain synergy. The different regions of the brain devoted to sight and sound activate to "turn on" more brain cells than if each area acted alone.

I'm not completely knocking repetition. No question about it, repetition is an important tool in enhancing memory. But too much of a good thing can be bad. Sometimes too much repetition can actually inhibit recall. In a research study in which volunteers were given lists of words to remember, one group was given a rehearsal strategy: They were told to repeat each word as many times as possible before the next word was given about six seconds later. The second group was asked simply to remember the words and wasn't given any tips or strategies about how to do so. The second group performed much better in recalling the words than did the first group. In other words, the frequency of the repetition interfered with the first-group's learning process.

In an interview with Gunther Karsten, the reigning German National Champion, who currently holds the world record for remembering random binary numbers (3,027 random binary digits given only thirty minutes of study time), I asked him how many times he repeated the numbers.

"Twice," he said.

How can anyone remember 3,027 of anything, especially binary numbers, after looking at them only a couple of times? Gunther simply uses the Law of Association to link new information, such as the list of binary numbers, with images and experiences that make sense to him. We'll get into more detail about how he does that later. The important thing to know now is that like most people with well-developed memories, Gunther is just an ordinary human being. He wasn't born with the gift of extraordinary memory, he simply trained the same memory that all of us have, and that training is *not* dependent on frequent repetition.

Mastering your memory means learning to minimize the drudgery of repetition. Going over and over material is an enormous waste of time, energy, and effort. In order for your memory to grow, you must give the information enough time to incubate. A farmer who plants seeds in the field does not immediately return to the spot. A wise farmer understands the development cycle of each crop and returns at the appointed time to cultivate the new growth. So it is with memory.

Treat repetition as a spice, using just enough to enhance memory. You can't get away from its use completely because it serves two important functions. First, it is an internal test to ensure that you have learned new information correctly. Perhaps you did not hear the name of the person you just met and ask for clarification: "I'm sorry, did you say your name was Bob or Rob?" Your original learning is increasing in strength as your memory grows stronger. If you learn something incorrectly, it will become more difficult to unlearn it.

A guest at a party that I attended was telling me the names of the other guests as they arrived. She mistakenly called one man Stephen Smith; I learned later that his real name was James. Now, every time I see this person, my inclination is to call him Stephen and not by his real name. It's been nearly impossible to correct that mistake. In fact, in my mind, I've given him a double name: Stephen James Smith. This is a code for me to know that emphasis should be on the second name, not the bogus first.

The second reason why repetition is important is that it is a tool to fight the primary enemy of memory — the passage of time.

Time is the ultimate memory eraser. In a classic experiment conducted by Hermann Ebbinghaus, the famed German experimental psychologist who lived at the turn of the twentieth century, he developed the first "forgetting curve." He discovered that memory decays dramatically soon after the original learning.

He compiled a list of nonsensical words such as ADH GBY and memorized them by the brute force of rote memory. Because the words did not mean anything, he was not able to apply the Three Reversible Rules of Engagement or the power of the "SEA to See" to strengthen the original learning. Also because the words were meaningless, they were not interesting, so by default, he was not able to apply the Law of Association to draw from previous knowledge. This is the worst-case scenario for learning and memory. However, it illustrates the whitewashing power of time.

After remembering a list of nonsensical words, he looked at how much he could remember over a wide range of times, and what he found was this: If he immediately repeated the words, he could remember 100 percent. If he waited twenty minutes, he could repeat 60 percent of the words. If he waited an hour, he could repeat only 45 percent of the words. Here are the results of this experiment:

Delay	Amount Remembered
Immediate	100%
20 minutes	60%
1 hour	45%
9 hours	35%
1 day	30%
2 days	25%
6 days	22%
30 days	20%

The power of time to decay and wipe away what we have learned is dramatic because it does it immediately. To interrupt the deleting process, here are five ways to strengthen memory:

Strengthen the degree of the original learning by applying the power of SEA to

See (Sensory, Emotion, and Action) to the material. On your mental palette there are not hundreds but thousands of senses and emotions you use to develop your mental eye. You make the images come alive by adding elements of sound, touch, or smell, which convert a two-dimensional portrait into an engaging experience. You are an artist as well as a composer. Use your new ability to create masterpieces of the mind.

Use the Law of Association to access the infinite storage capacity of your brain and draw on what you already know. You accelerate your learning process by reflecting the way your neurons connect. You take what your brain does at the microscopic level, associate individual brain cells, and use that same process to associate new material with the millions of facts, figures, and experiences that you've already retained in your long-term memory.

The Fuzzy Fifteen

Maximize your memory by breaking up the study time. The longer you study something without review, the less you will be able to recall.

Try this exercise on a few volunteers or

have someone try it on you. Ask the volunteers (or be prepared yourself) to remember as many numbers in order as possible. Read aloud the following twenty-digit number at the rate of one digit per second. Then, go back to the beginning of the list and see how many are remembered. As soon as most of the group falters, immediately ask them to repeat the very last digit, then the next-to-last digit, and so on until blanks are drawn.

13145926535897932384

You will find that memory is strong for the first four to seven digits. This is the "primacy effect." We tend to remember things at the very beginning of a study period. Some may be able to remember the last one or two digits. This is the "recency effect," as we also tend to remember a few things at the end. It is all the information in the middle that tends to drop away. The longer the list, the more information we forget. It has nothing to do with understanding, but everything to do with memory.

If we shorten the list, our recall goes up dramatically. By breaking up the study time, we can increase our memory during the learning period. Because our attention span varies depending on the material we are trying to commit to memory, the length of the learning period is highly subjective. What we're trying to achieve is deliberate intensity. It may surprise you to learn that it took only eleven minutes to fly to the moon in the late 1960s. Although it took the astronauts three days to reach the moon after blasting off from Earth, the rocket fuel burned for only eleven minutes to generate enough intensity to overcome the force of gravity. Once in space, the *Apollo* craft needed little effort to fly to the moon. So it is with memory. It is that intense focus in the first few seconds that makes for little effort after time passes.

Try using the TV formula to pattern your study habits. Most television programs are no longer than an hour, and that should be your maximum limit for any single sitting. You may find that the commercials often begin after the first fifteen minutes of a one-hour program, so try using that as a baseline. I find that a minimum of fifteen minutes and a maximum of one hour before continuing to the final two stages works about right.

Review the material until you can repeat it once without an error, wait thirty seconds to a minute, and repeat it again. If you are successful on the second repetition, this marks the end of your study period. If you are unsuccessful, repeat it again after thirty seconds to a minute have passed. The first time you are able to do it perfectly ensures that you are processing the correct information. The second time you repeat it is the confidence factor and marks the end of your study time. Here is a great study tip: If it is a list or a group of people's names you are learning, repeat the list backward the second time. We naturally retain more at the beginning. So when we start at the end of the list and work our way back, it helps to capture the middle information before it quickly falls away. Also, give yourself a positive affirmation about developing the virtually perfect nature of your memory. The mind is marvelous but we have subconsciously sabotaged its ability because we tend to dwell on the negative — that is, the number of things that we have forgotten. Very rarely do we dwell on how much we do remember. Positive affirmation helps us reinforce the marvelous power of the mind.

Let ten to fifteen minutes pass, then repeat the material once without looking at the original material. The moment your study period ends, the information begins to transfer from your working memory to your long-term memory. I envision this process as kindergarten children standing in line waiting to get into the classroom after recess. They are all excited and bubbling with energy and, without proper supervision, some children may get out of line and get lost somewhere down the hall. It is the nature of children to become easily distracted, and the last thing they want to do is stand in line. It's the same with memory. There is something about the nature of memory during that ten-to-fifteen-minute processing time that encourages information to get lost.

In 2002 our daughter, Kristen, lapsed into a coma as the result of what we now believe was viral encephalitis that had infected her brain. The virus caused her brain to expand and formed temporary lesions in areas of her brain affecting motor control and memory centers. During the recovery process, she would ask us how all of this had happened, we would tell her, then in about ten to fifteen minutes she would ask the question again, having no knowledge of having asked it the first time. She is now fully recovered and living a very healthy, blessed life. The temporary damage to her brain blocked the entry of information into her long-term memory while she was ill. After about ten to fifteen minutes, the information dissipated. This incident gives a very powerful clue to the length of time it takes to process information between your working memory and your long-term memory. If you can remember something for fifteen minutes, you can be reasonably confident that it is on its way to your long-term-storage areas.

Dominic O'Brien, the eight-time World Memory Champion, is not only a friend of mine, he is one of my memory mentors. He has one of the best-developed memories in the world and can remember eighteen to twenty decks of playing cards in an hour. What is interesting is that he does not commit to memory all eighteen decks of cards at one time. He breaks the memorization process into three increments, with each increment consisting of the memorization of six decks. What this means is that he will commit to memory one deck of cards, then the second deck of cards, then the third deck, and so on until he memorizes the sixth deck. Amazingly, it takes Dominic a little over two minutes to remember a single deck of cards in this event, so by the time he memorizes the sixth deck, approximately twelve to fifteen minutes have passed since he looked at the first deck. At this point, he stops any further memorization and goes back to the first deck for a quick review, then the second deck, the third, and so on until he has reviewed the sixth deck. Then he begins the second increment, which consists of decks seven through twelve and repeats the memorization and review process.

"I refer to my review as the 'spinning plate phenomenon,'" he explains. "Imagine spinning six plates, one at a time, on six sticks. By the time you reach the sixth plate, the first plate is losing some of its momentum and it needs additional spins. With memory, by the time I reach the sixth deck, the first deck is losing some of its momentum, it's becoming a little fuzzy, and so I go back to give it a quick mental boost."

As you are learning or memorizing new information, you need to ensure that the material is not becoming fuzzy on its way to your long-term memory. A quick review around the fifteen-minute mark will help keep the data from getting lost. The next time you meet a group of people, surreptitiously set the alarm on your watch or keep an eye on the clock to see if you can still repeat their names after the first quarter hour.

The Rule of Ones

Conquering the "fuzzy fifteen" is a great first step to committing information to your long-term memory. When you have successfully repeated the material you are trying to learn after fifteen minutes have passed, you have reached the end of your learning period. However, because Father Time has an obsessive-compulsive habit of wanting to clean information from your mental hard drive, you should consider establishing a periodic review routine called the Rule of Ones. Basically, it is a review that begins at the end of your learning period and consists of five specific time frames — one hour, one day, one week, one month, and one-quarter of a year.

To understand how this works, let's return for a moment to the five basic questions that you can ask any person to get to know more about him or her. That was in chapter 3. Do you remember what they are? Do you still see the icon you created in your mind? If you can, great! If you can't, now is the time to turn frustration into fascination. First, remind yourself that there is nothing wrong with your ability to recall information. You do that perfectly, every day. The words on this page, the sound of the ringing telephone, and the smell of roses are evidence of this truth. Second, remind yourself that time works very quickly to erase data from your brain, as evident from the Ebbinghaus experiment. If you can't remember, you probably have allowed too much time to pass before you thought about it again. The Rule of Ones helps keep information from getting lost in the land of forgetfulness.

Let's take an example of how this can work for you. Suppose you are trying to remember the eight building blocks of life, called the Bagua, from the ancient Chinese art of feng shui. They are health, love, wealth, career, wisdom, reputation, children, and helpful people. Use the SEA to See method to create an image or experience in your mind that contains all eight building blocks, as we did together for the five basic questions. After you have painted this masterpiece in your mind, ensure that you really know the material by repeating the list forward and backward. Do this twice. Now, set a timer for fifteen minutes and do something creative in the interim.

Get your mind completely off the list, though this may be harder to do than you think. When the timer goes off, repeat the list. One successful repetition, either backward or forward, marks the end of your learning period. If you forget some of the items, don't worry.

Sometimes, it is as if information enters our brain, and time acts like an acid to dissolve that data, leaving only fragments of the original learning. This happens to all of us, even to the very best memorizers in the world. But you can turn it to your advantage! During a live interview on CNN's *Anderson Cooper 360°* in May 2004, I was reciting a deck of cards when, to my horror, I drew a blank. I forgot the thirteenth card — the five of spades. That was a long time ago, yet I still — and always will — remember that specific card because I forgot it. Turn your own frustration into fascination by understanding that those things we first forget may in the long run be the things we best remember.

Now, let one day pass, then repeat the information once without looking at the original material. Remind yourself that your ability to recall information is never the issue. If you have forgotten anything, don't be discouraged, because decay is a fact of life. It is a fact of memory. The power of time is strong enough to erase 70 to 80 percent of what we learned after a single day. The key is to analyze why you forgot something. You may have forgotten because the strength of your original learning was compromised in the memory process. Sometimes the initial embedding, or encoding, may not have been intense enough. Think what would have happened if the *Saturn* rocket motors hadn't burned for the full eleven minutes necessary to escape Earth's gravity. The rocket, like a compromised memory, would have failed.

Whatever it is you have forgotten, return to the SEA (Sensory, Emotion, and Action) to See method and add one and only one perfect SEA element to rejuvenate the data and make it whole again. For instance, suppose you can't remember the third Bagua block, which is "wealth." Instead of just seeing a bag of coins, you may want to add the sound of the coins hitting the floor. The reason it is so important to add only one element at a time is that the brain is very efficient. It needs only a few clues to trigger the entire memory.

Let one week pass, then repeat the information.

It may seem that a week is too long since

your last review and renewal session. But look again at the results of the Ebbinghaus experiment. The amount of material forgotten begins to level out after the initial steep decline. The strength of the original learning that has been reinforced after the twenty-four-hour renewal remains intact after a week has gone by.

Contestants who participate in the World Memory Championships understand this phenomenon very well. One of the events in the tournament is to commit to memory as many random digits (1, 4, 2, 0, 8, etc.) as possible within one hour. This is a fiendishly clever test. Since the goal is to remember more numbers than your competitor, you need to keep the repetition of the number sequences to a minimum. The more time a contestant takes to review the sequence, the less time there is to commit additional numbers to memory. At the end of the hour, contestants are given two hours to recall the hundreds of numbers they have remembered in perfect sequence. If you wait one week and ask a contestant to repeat the sequence of numbers learned seven days before, he or she is likely to remember 95 to 100 percent of the numbers. This is an amazing process and one you simply have to experience to believe. Put a reminder on your calendar at the end of seven days to see how many of the eight blocks of the Bagua you can remember. If you're wondering why a book about improving your memory is telling you to put a reminder on your calendar, see the accompanying sidebar!

Repeating the information you have learned at the one-week interval interrupts the decay process and keeps most of it in your memory for approximately one month. What little bit of information you have forgotten will quickly be renewed at the one-month-review mark.

After one month, repeat the information yet again. This is the point at which students in high school or college can really find immense benefits. By following the Rule of Ones, they will have already invested sufficient time and energy into memory that only a brief review of the accumulated material is necessary the night before an exam. Isn't it much more efficient to invest small amounts of time and effort over a long period than to try to cram as much as possible the night before?

The fifth and final review should take place after one-quarter of a year (three months). This helps to solidify it into your long-term memory.

Remembering the Future

So what's with the calendar reminder? Doesn't a developed memory help me remember when to do things?

Simply put, no!

Time and memory are like oil and water: They don't mix and they don't work well together. Memory, in some ways, supersedes time. In one moment you are in the present, and the next instant you can take your mind back to when you were five years old. You can sift through decades in just a few seconds. You can relive an experience in a fraction of the time it took for the experience to develop, like the first time you were able to ride a bike or you drove a car by yourself. However, trying to remember to do things in the future is a bit of an oxymoron. By definition, the event has not yet happened. Psychologists refer to this as "prospective memory." The only reliable way to remember to do something in the future, like stop by the grocery store and pick up that gallon of milk, is to have an external memory aid of some kind that activates at the exact time you need to complete the task. Use of electronic personal-data assistants (PDAs) is one of the better ways to do this, because they can be programmed to alarm you at the proper time with sufficient information to give you an idea of why the device went off in the first place — i.e., "pick up milk."

These devices are good for appointment and meeting reminders and for taking medications. Another example is the alarm clock you use every day to help remind you to get out of bed at a particular time. If it fails and you are late to work, the boss does not accuse you of having a poor memory. You needed that external reminder to interrupt what you were doing at the moment — in this case, sleeping — and alter your present course of action. So it is with trying to remember things to do in the future. You need some type of external reminder to coincide with the right event at the right time. Don't let the perception of a poor prospective memory delude you into thinking that you have a bad memory. These are two completely separate concepts that have nothing to do with each other.

In formulating the Rule of Ones I found that daily, weekly, monthly, and quarterly reviews work best for me. But they are just suggested frequencies. Use them only as a template to set up your personal renewal process. Highly complex information may require an increase in frequency or it may not. Before spending additional hours reviewing material, try shortening the learning period first, then begin the Rule of Ones.

To make the best use of your renewal process, take a ten- to fifteen-minute break after you are able to repeat the material twice. Use that break period to study additional material or to do something creative and innovative. The important thing is to use that time to allow the information to seep its way into your memory bank without your disturbing it. Allow the information to be incubated. Become a wise farmer.

When you begin to memorize something, set a goal for how long you want to remember the material. Be realistic. You won't need to recall a grocery list a year from now, nor will you need to know the dates of important battles in history ten years from now. It's impossible to remember everything, no matter how exciting, interesting, engaging, or important the material is. If you could do that, you would have a photographic memory, and we know how terrible that would be. What you are developing is your own perfect memory, one that is well balanced with valuable information of your choice that helps you become more extraordinary than you already are.

Repetition has its place in forming our memories, but there are other, more important tools at our command, including the ability to receive, retain, and recall information. If you understand and are developing the SEA to See concept by implementing the Three Reversible Rules of Engagement, then you are already in the process of maximizing your ability to receive information. The ability to retain more of what you receive requires a two-step process that links your working memory with your long-term memory. Your working memory has a very small storage space, but your long-term memory has infinite capacity. If you are practicing and developing the art of association, then you are completing the first step (the second step will be introduced in the next chapter). When we say that we want to improve our memory, what we are really

saying is that we want to maximize our recall, preferably with a minimum amount of
effort.

The brain agrees!

Chapter Six
Discovering the Roman Room

Have you ever looked up a phone number and then had a problem remembering it long enough to get to the phone and dial it? That used to be one of my most vexing memory failings. It's amazing how fast seven little numbers can just evaporate out of your mind. This is an example of what psychologists call our "working memory." It is the part of your mind that holds a small amount of information for only a few seconds, and it is very fragile.

Your ability to retain information is dependent on two capacities of your brain with very different sizes — your working memory and your long-term memory. To use an analogy, your working memory is like an uncharted island of unknown size. If seconds are like feet and minutes are like miles, your island of working memory may be only a few feet wide, or it may be several miles around. The size depends on your natural abilities and your natural inclinations. For example, if you are good at remembering lots of names and faces, your island is very wide. But if you're terrible at remembering numbers, your island is only a few feet across. The size of your island appears to expand or contract depending on what you're trying to remember. Frustrating, isn't it?

Your long-term memory, on the other hand, is like the continent, full of resources and virtually unlimited storage capacity. Unlike the little island of your working memory, your long-term memory never decreases in size.

In 2003, Dominic O'Brien set a Guinness World Record by remembering fifty-four decks of playing cards, all shuffled together, after only a single sighting of each card. This task would seem humanly impossible unless Dominic had a photographic memory, which he readily admitted he doesn't. Indeed, Dominic suffered from dyslexia as a child. He performed so poorly in school that he eventually dropped out. So how could he remember over twenty-eight hundred cards after seeing them only once? Why didn't his memory crash under the weight of fifty-four decks?

Dominic and others like him have learned to do something extraordinary with their minds. They have learned to build a bridge between the paucity of their working memory and the near-infinite storage capacity of their long-term memory. Surprisingly, this bridge building isn't some modern development of memory experts using magnetic resonance imaging and other high-tech methods. It's an ancient secret, discovered over twenty-five hundred years ago, but it has been mostly ignored in this modern age.

The History of the Roman Room

Legend has it that the poet Simonides recited a soliloquy for a banquet held in one of the great halls in ancient Greece. Shortly after he left the building, the roof caved in, killing everyone inside. The bodies were so mangled they could not be recognized and authorities went to Simonides to see if he could remember at least who some of the people were. Surprisingly, he was able to recall everyone in the hall simply by remembering where the person sat around the tables in the room. He remembered them by their location.

The Roman orator Cicero, around the turn of the first century, expanded this concept by mentally placing ideas around the tables instead of people. He could recite volumes of information by seeing visions and symbols in the chairs. Like the icons that we have on our computer desktop screens, his mental icons represented the critical points he needed to recall in his arguments or debates. Cicero became world renowned for his ability to make clear, lucid points in his debates without using notes. This technique became known as the Roman Room method. By projecting onto his mental screen a room equipped with tables and chairs, Cicero could simply walk around the area in his mind and elaborate his key points. He organized information in his mind so that he could mentally go around any table picking up the memories he had stored in various chairs and simply describing those memories to his audience. Having worked through the previous exercises in this book, you already know that you have an infinite SEA of knowledge in your brain and are capable of storing vast amounts of data in your memory. So the real question is not, "Do I have the information inside my head?" but rather, "Where is it located?"

Using the Roman Room technique to expand your memory is much akin to the simple solution that my wife, Janet, found for my perennial problem of lost car keys. She created for me a "forget-me-not" spot, specifically the top dresser drawer. Now, instead of putting down the keys any old place when I come in from the garage — and then spending hours looking all over the house for them the next time I want to go somewhere — I just drop them in the top drawer of the dresser. It's become a habit, I don't even have to think about it, and I always know where my keys are. Trying to find keys is a waste of time and energy. It increases stress and it makes you doubt your intelligence. So it is with an unorganized memory. We have already talked about ways to focus your memory. Combining focus with the Roman Room method of organization improves the power of your memory by orders of magnitude.

Creating Your First Roman Room

Cicero created a kind of forget-me-not spot using his natural surroundings. I began in my living room. For you, it can begin in the room where you are now. When I look around my area, I initially see a lot of "stuff." I see stereo speakers that were long-ago graduation presents, a TV console, a fireplace, my favorite reclining chair, a rocking chair, a lamp table, a coffee table, a sleeper sofa, and recessed lights in the ceiling near the ceiling fan. When we first moved into our home, Janet and I — to be honest, mostly Janet — gave careful attention to where each piece of furniture should be located for practicality, to maximize the overall look and feel of the room, and to use the floor space most efficiently. In fact, what looks like random order is actually well organized because of its location. Perhaps that is part of the appeal of such shows as *Extreme Makeover* and magazines like *Architectural Digest.* Ordinary homeowners can get ideas from people who have a knack for designing rooms that are both functional and aesthetically pleasing. It astounds me that the basic components of a room — four corners, four walls, a floor, and a ceiling — can be so completely transformed that no two rooms are identical. There seems to be an infinite number of arrangements to a room's basic components, and this is the ultimate secret to your mental organizational tool. Once again, an infinite number is captured by a finite arrangement — just like the brain.

When I look carefully at our living room from the doorway, over to my left is the speaker stand in the corner. The TV console is located along the adjacent wall, and the rocking chair is in the next corner of the room. The fireplace is located on the wall opposite the doorway, and my favorite chair is located in the third corner of the room. The third wall is actually a larger doorway that leads to the dining room, and a lamp table occupies the fourth corner. Along the fourth and final wall is the sleeper sofa. The floor, carpeted, has a large walnut coffee table in front of the sofa, and a fan hangs from the ceiling.

Each of these room components is in a very specific place and each component is connected to the other by the shape of the room. Looking at the room as a house designer might look, in a clockwise fashion, I go corner–wall–corner–wall–corner–wall–corner–wall–floor–ceiling. Each room component is located in a very specific position that can be numbered for easy identification. When I walk into the room, stereo speakers are located in the corner to my left. This is position number 1. The television console is along the adjacent wall. That is position number 2. The rocking chair is in the next corner (going clockwise around the room), which is position 3. I continue in this manner, noting what object is located in which position around the room until I come to the ceiling fan, which is in position 10.

The chart below summarizes this.

Position	Location	Object
1	corner	speaker
2	wall	TV console
3	corner	rocking chair
4	wall	fireplace
5	corner	recliner
6	wall	doorway
7	corner	lamp table
8	wall	sleeper sofa
9	floor	coffee table
10	ceiling	ceiling fan

If I close my eyes, I can see this room completely in my mind. If I apply the third Reversible Rule of Engagement and give action to the picture in my mind, I can move the lens of my mind's eye — just like Ken Burns does in his excellent documentaries, beginning with the speaker and moving the camera lens all the way around the room, seeing each object in its very specific location.

Of all the exercises we have done up to this point, this is one of the most important, because you have to do it to believe that you can. The power of this tool, its depth and magnitude, cannot be fully appreciated until you experience it for yourself.

I've identified seven points that will make it easier for you to apply the Roman Room organizational method.

First, the order and pattern that you see in the room, both with your physical eye and your mental eye, is very important. The left side of your brain needs order, logic, sequence, and numbers to function. The natural layout of any room satisfies this requirement.

Second, nearly every room contains four walls, four corners, a floor, and a ceiling. That makes it easy to set up a numbering sequence for any room. Always begin with the corner located over your left shoulder when you enter the room. That will always be position 1. For example, my living room begins with the speaker in position 1. The next room I enter, the dining room, contains an antique sewing box in the corner just over my left shoulder. That is position 11. The next room, the kitchen, contains a set of wooden TV trays in the corner over my left shoulder. That is position 21.

Third, visualize a single detail about whatever object occupies each position in a room, focusing on some small detail that will always bring the object into clear focus. I see the manufacturer's logo on the speaker, the curve of the wooden television console, and the color of the checked plaid blanket hanging on the rocking chair. If there is nothing in the corner, look at the molding or the walls very carefully for small imperfections. Any kind of detail is significant and will remain fixed in your mind. If no imperfection exists in your corner, pick any random portable object in the house and temporarily place it in the corner.

Fourth, dust the room. (Guys, your wives will love you for this, though they may look at you a little strangely.) One of the best ways to seal each object and its position into your mind is to dust it with a feather duster or a cloth. You're interacting with the object and transforming it into an experience. Use windows, light switches, paintings, carpet, whatever happens to be there. Make a table, like the accompanying one, for whatever room you are in right now.

Fifth, take a number. Take ten pieces of scrap paper and number them 1 through 10. Put the scraps in a hat and draw one. Let's say you draw the 5. Start counting from position 1 (over your left shoulder when you enter the room) and move sequentially to position 5. That should be the corner in front of you to your right as you enter the room. Note the object that is in position 5. Repeat this exercise at least five times and you will begin to see how quickly your eyes and your mind adapt to the pattern. After a few more repetitions, it will become automatic. If you draw the number 10, your eyes will immediately go to the ceiling.

Sixth, develop your mental picture. After you have completed the number-drawing exercise, relax for ten to fifteen minutes or do something completely off task: read, take a walk, work on a crossword puzzle, make a phone call, whatever. Then, wherever you are, close your eyes and re-create the room in your mind. Slowly count forward, 1 through 10, seeing each object in your mind, then count backward, again seeing each object, until you reach number 1.

Finally, seventh, repeat the number-drawing process, but this time speed up your counting. You will see how quickly your mental picture begins to spin in your mind.

Once you have completed these seven steps, this room will never change in your mind. It has become a permanent mental drawer into which you can place anything that you want to remember. To truly understand the power of this method, it is best to put it to use right away. You can, of course, employ this method right away to memorize any list of things you wish.

Using the Roman Room

This powerful memory technique is a five-step strategy that can be applied to any list. Review The 10 Steps of Mental Fitness in the sidebar on pages 156–159, then follow this outline.

Step A

Condense the information in the list into its simplest form, usually a concrete word or idea that naturally brings to mind a tangible picture or an engaging experience.

That's SEA at work. Let your brain work naturally. For example, I would think *book* as a condensed form of the first step to mental fitness, reading analytically and critically. If you see a picture of the word *book* in your mind, stop there. At least for now, don't try to add more bits of information. While it's better to generate your own list, here is mine as an example.

1. *Book* for reading critically.
2. *Left hand* for using your nondominant hand.
3. *Diary* for keeping a journal.
4. *Crossword* for doing crossword puzzles.
5. *Dictionary* for expanding your vocabulary.
6. *Brain* for doing memory exercises.
7. *Chess* for playing strategy games.
8. *Barbells* for getting physical exercise.
9. *Instrument* for learning to play music.
10. *Language* for learning a foreign language.

Step B

Apply the Law of Association and associate each image in the list with an object in the room you're in. You can't help but do this. The Law of Association is very clear: Any two objects automatically associate with each other. Look at the room around you again. Now, mentally place a book in the first corner sitting on the object that is in the corner. For me, I see a book sitting on top of the speaker. Move to position 2 in the room — for me, that's the television console — and place the next object, a left hand, there. I see myself changing the TV channel using my left hand. Now to position 3 in the room, which for me is the rocking chair. I see an open diary in my own handwriting sitting on the rocking chair. Continue around the room in this manner, placing some visualization of each of The 10 Steps of Mental Fitness in the appropriate location.

Step C

As you place your visualization of each step in its location, analyze the interaction of the objects. This will often enhance the image because you are asking who, what, why, and how. Sometimes the logical side of your brain wants to dissolve the image because it doesn't make sense. For instance, why would I want to exercise on the couch, which is the object in position 8 in my room? If I jogged my 200-plus-pound frame on the couch, it would break. But isn't that interesting? Breaking the couch by jogging on it makes a powerful association more memorable because the two images are interacting with each other to create a third.

A similar interaction might have occurred to you when I said I saw my open diary on the rocking chair. You may want to ask, "Why would someone leave an open diary sitting on the rocking chair? Perhaps he or she was rocking away, thinking deep thoughts, and then got called away. I wonder what it says. I wonder if I am in it. Should I read it, or should I respect the author's privacy?"

Step D

Be creative in finding ways to strengthen the association. It is the strength and vividness of the association that enables recall, not the number of repetitions. For instance, what do language and a ceiling fan have in common? You might imagine foreign-language books or tapes sitting atop the fan as it is spinning. Or you might see that the installation instructions for the ceiling fan are written in another language and taped to the fan. You might notice that the name of the lightbulb manufacturer is not clear because the heat from the bulb has faded the inscription, causing the words to look like they were written in another language. Now the association is complete.

This may seem like a lot of additional work. But the fact is that you're saving tremendous amounts of time and effort that would otherwise have to be invested in multiple repetitions of the information you want to remember. Research studies show that even after reviewing a sequential list of words seventeen times, you still have only a 75 percent probability of remembering the sixth, seventh, and eighth words. But more important, it is another way to expand your imagination and your creativity.

Step E

Return to the numbered scraps of paper we used earlier in this chapter to learn to automatically identify each location in a room. Pick a number out of the hat. See if you remember which mental fitness tip corresponds to the number you are seeing.

Prepare to be amazed! You will find, in a very short time, that you are able to remember every item not only in sequential order, but in any order, backward or forward.

This process takes about ten minutes to complete. After introducing this method and discussing how to remember The 10 Steps of Mental Fitness, one seventy-year-old lady, in a small church outside of Winston-Salem, North Carolina, told me, "I wouldn't have believed it if I hadn't just experienced it."

The Roman Room is highly effective because it utilizes familiar surroundings. We live in a ten-room home, if I count all the bathrooms and the garage. Thus, with ten items per room, I have one hundred places that I see every day that do not change and are constantly reinforced. I use most of the rooms for transient storage of material in my mind. For instance, if I read a magazine or a newspaper that has five or ten bits of information that I want to remember, I will temporarily place these in one room. There are some rooms in my home where I have "permanent storage" because some advice or thoughts are too important to forget. Thus, in the spare bedroom upstairs, I have stored in my mind the five motivating factors of life — guilt, fear, anger, approval, materialism — and the five reasons for finding purpose in life — meaning, focus, simplification, motivation, and preparation.

But we aren't confined merely to the rooms in the places we live. Otherwise, some New Yorkers living in studio co-op apartments would be confined to just two rooms, the living/bedroom and the bathroom. I maintain a mental list of homes that I know very well where I keep other material in permanent storage. These homes include my grandparents', the home in which I was raised, the three apartments I lived in during my college years, and some of our close friends' homes. If you live in a one-bedroom apartment, don't despair. Use the lobby of your building as a storage area, or perhaps use your office. Any location with which you're sufficiently familiar will work, even a closet. Once you've set these places in your memory, visit them mentally from time to time, perhaps during your commute to work or during a TV commercial, and reacquaint yourself with what's stored there. Those places and memories are now part of your long-term memory. Because it is so well organized, you'll know exactly where to go if you need to remember something specific.

Dr. Sanjay Gupta, senior medical correspondent for CNN, aired an interview with me in March 2005. After explaining the Roman Room method to him, he picked out ten places in the TV studio. I showed him ten cards from a shuffled deck, which he then associated with the ten locations in the studio. He recalled every card in perfect order. The whole process took less than fifteen minutes. It was delightful to watch and experience. "If I can do this, anyone can," he enthused.

Exactly!

Just in case you think you will run out of rooms quickly, don't despair. As we discussed in chapter 3, your memory is virtually picture perfect. If you get a chance, flip through one of the many home-and-garden magazines or, better yet, *Architectural Digest.* Now that you understand the concept of the Roman Room, you need not actually live there in order to use it. In the World Memory Championships, some of the hour-long events require that I place things I want to remember in a lot of rooms. For example, when I am trying to remember at least one thousand items in

The 10 Steps of Mental Fitness

A powerful memory helps define who we are. Yet, how much time do we actually spend exercising our memory? We don't think twice about going to the fitness center and spending thirty minutes running on a treadmill that doesn't take us anywhere. When it comes to our physical health, it is the journey, not the destination, that's important. So it is with memory. Studies indicate that by doing these activities at least four times a week, a person may reduce the risk of contracting Alzheimer's disease when compared to someone who doesn't do them at all.

1. Read critically and analytically. Stop every so often in the text and ask questions. What is the author trying to say? What are the names of the characters? What are their backgrounds? What are their relationships? How is this going to affect the outcome? Periodic review during the reading reinforces memory by keeping facts, events, and character details fresh in the mind.

2. Use your nondominant hand more frequently. Remember, the left side of your brain controls the right side of your body, and vice versa. If you're right handed, try dialing a phone number with your left hand or brushing your teeth with your left hand. You will find that you almost have to rethink how to do it. These activities help to strengthen cognitive connections.

3. Keep a diary. We have already explored the value of keeping a journal. We also help refine our thinking as we organize our thoughts and put them down in a logical pattern that makes sense to us, or to anyone else with whom you care to share the diary.

4. Do a crossword puzzle. It doesn't have to be a particularly difficult puzzle. What you're doing is using the left side of your brain to logically process the clues, then the right side of your brain assembles the clues to achieve what scientists call the "aha! moment." On magnetic resonance images, a sudden flicker on the right side of the brain occurs when the answer to a puzzle has been found.

5. Expand your vocabulary. A large vocabulary improves a person's creative process and helps to break down social and business barriers, which are often built with a specialized lexicon. More important, a large vocabulary helps you interpret the world around you — helps you distill down complex thoughts and ideas into single words and phrases. The purpose of a large vocabulary is not to impress but to interpret.

6. Improve your memory. We're already doing that, of course, but there are memory games and exercises beyond those in this book. Playing Hasbro Games' Simon is an entertaining way to exercise your memory.

7. Take up chess, checkers, or other games of strategy. These games improve our spatial awareness, logic, pattern identification, imagination, and creativity.

8. Exercise. That's right, physical exercise clearly helps our mental processes. People who engage in regular aerobic exercise report that their planning is easier, their attention is more focused, and they suffer less stress.

9. Take up a musical instrument. You don't have to aspire to be in a rock band, just take on the challenge of learning to play an instrument. Studies of musicians' brain cells show that they have up to ten thousand dendrites on each cell, a tribute to the complexity of learning how to read, interpret, and play music.

10. Learn a language. Again, you don't have to aspire to become fluent. Learning another language involves multiple uses of several brain skills and areas, including vocabulary, auditory skills, imagination, reading, and many others.

---

sequential order, I need to remember at least one hundred rooms. Amazingly, I have never even set foot in any of them. The closest I ever got was my fingertips on the page of the magazine. The reason is simple: The mind doesn't distinguish between what is real and what is vividly imagined. In my mind there is no difference between looking at a room while standing in the doorway or looking at a room while seeing it on the page. To make the room vivid, I mentally dust the room (my wife will tell you that I do a lot more imaginary dusting than I do real dusting). If it's appropriate, I mentally pick up each object, like a vase on a stand, and note its shape, texture, and feel while dusting it with a mental cloth. If it is something like a fireplace or a painting on the wall, I still take my cloth and feel the subtle grooves in the mantel or in the picture frame. Again, I am noting and picking out detail and applying deliberate intensity to each location in the room. Sometimes I even use aromatherapy or light a scented candle to help establish in my mind the overall environment of each room. Smell is a powerful memory stimulant, and it adds to the vividness of the environment. When you apply this technique, you understand how unlimited your mind and memory can be, because there are an infinite number of pictures of rooms in a seemingly infinite number of magazines on the bookshelves each month.

Chapter Seven
Remembering Names and Faces

Let's face it, some of our most uncomfortable and embarrassing moments occur when we come face-to-face with people and find that we have forgotten their names. I don't know if it's worse to have forgotten the name altogether or to call them by some name other than their own. Names in the English language are difficult to remember because they are arbitrary. They don't define who we are. Take my name, for instance. I'm not really a Scotsman and I don't live in a forest of hags. I know a fellow named Tim Baker, a mechanical engineer at the local textile plant. He likes to play golf and enjoys watching basketball. But if you had just been introduced to him, you'd know virtually nothing about him. Yet, if he told you that he ran a bakery, you would immediately know much more about him. This is what psychologists call the Baker/baker paradox. The name Baker doesn't mean anything, but the word *baker* taps directly into the information bank that is your long-term memory. We'll use the paradox shortly to help you recall names. But first I want to show you how many people you know whom you don't know you know. We'll compile an inventory of fairly common names and see if that list jogs your memory circuits.

First, dash up to the attic or down to the basement and grab a few of your old high-school yearbooks. You literally spent the formative years of your life in school and were in close contact with hundreds of classmates whom you think you've forgotten. Thumbing through these school pictures will not only bring back a flood of "forgotten" memories, it will begin to give you a sense of how many people you really do know. It's a good warm-up exercise because you're putting a familiar name with a familiar face.

The second thing I want you to do, the next time you're in a bookstore or library, is to pick up one of the many name-your-baby books that are published. Don't buy it, just spend a few minutes flipping through it. Although there will be lots of names you won't recognize, there will be a staggering number of names that will leap to mind when you read them, triggering memories that you didn't realize you had. Also note that when you are doing this, usually only one person comes to mind at a time for each familiar name. That's the mind at work: one thought at a time. Instead of trying to conjure up memories of every James you know, just move on to the next name on the list. You'll often find that other people named James will come floating into your mind.

Now look at the chart at the end of this chapter, which lists the twenty most-popular names in 1963, derived from the Social Security Administration (for a much more extensive list of popular names, go to the Social Security Web site, www.ssa.gov, and click on the "Social Security Delivers the Most Popular Names" link). These are the names of people you're most likely to meet, and knowing many people by the same name will also help you remember, for reasons that will be revealed shortly.

If you have access to the Internet you should also visit the Web site for the U.S. Census Bureau, www.census.gov, and click on the genealogy link. There you will find the one thousand most-common surnames in the United States, according to the latest census. Print them out and keep them with your daily journal.

Finally, at the library or bookstore, take a look at *The People's Almanac.* This is an extensive resource list of actors and actresses, Academy Award winners through the years, and popular television shows and music icons. It's a veritable Who's Who in Entertainment. Remember, the people you "know" aren't just those with whom you work or socialize. You also "know" Jennifer Aniston, Halle Berry, and Nicole Kidman. (Does this list suggest that a male compiled it?)

By the time you've completed these relatively simple exercises, I think you'll be convinced that you know many more people than you thought you did. More important, however, you've just woven some neural nets, the brain-cell alignments that form a specific pattern that allows you to "see" a person in your mind's eye. That's an important foundation for learning to remember more names and faces. To use an analogy, imagine that you are a fisherman on an island. You are making neural nets and casting them into the sea to retrieve names and faces.

Before you begin this next practice strategy, I want you to think about some of the mental tools that you use to create an environment when you are introduced to someone for the first time. You probably don't realize that you create such an environment, but you do. That environment is a crucial part of the strategy for remembering names. If you can re-create the surroundings where the memory was first made, your chances of recall dramatically improve.

What does your personal environment consist of? It varies from person to person, but it's safe to say that most people smile when meeting someone for the first time. You probably also extend your hand in a gesture indicating that you wish to shake the person's hand. If you're particularly effusive, you may also grab the person's arm with your left hand. If you're in Hollywood, you may even hug the person.

Finally, you usually say something. It may be something as simple as "Nice to meet you," or you could go into more detail, such as "Where do you work?" or "Do you live around here?" or "Aren't you Sally's mother?"

All the while that you're creating the physical environment in which you're meeting a new person, you're consciously or unconsciously making mental notes about the person. Usually the most striking aspect of the person creates the first mental note. It might be his eyes, his hair, or even his voice that makes a first impression, but something almost certainly strikes you about the person. Thus, the "first-meeting environment" usually consists of smiles, handshakes, a little small talk, and a mental appraisal of the person you're meeting.

The accompanying table contains the top ten names of boys and girls for 1963. As you look at each name, recall someone you know with the same name. Write down a few characteristics about that particular person, such as the color of her hair, her eyes, her physical build, her job, and her hobbies or interests. If no one comes to mind right away, don't worry about it. There will be other practice sessions, strategies, and hints to help your name database grow in this chapter. You'll probably find that within a few minutes of completing this exercise, you'll begin remembering people with these names. We'll talk more about this weird little phenomenon, but for now just be aware that it's very common.

Top Ten Baby Names in 1963

Male	Characteristics	Female	Characteristics
Michael		Lisa	
John		Mary	
David		Susan	
James		Karen	
Robert		Linda	
Mark		Donna	
William		Patricia	
Richard		Lori	
Thomas		Sandra	
Jeffrey		Cynthia	

In doing that last exercise, you may have found that you didn't immediately recall anyone named Michael, but that while you were pondering any Roberts you might know, a Michael or two popped unexpectedly into your mind. That happened because you launched a neural net in your brain and it simply took a little while for the net to hoist out a name. Think of the process as if it is a train on a track. You started your train on the Michael track, and as you were traveling along the track, Michaels started climbing aboard. It just took them a few minutes to get to the tracks after they heard the train coming. As you regularly practice this and similar exercises, you'll be amazed by how full your "train" becomes.

Names and Associations

The secret of remembering names lies in the effective use of the Law of Association. Recall that any two things can be associated. The trick is to find the best and most efficient way to associate a new name with something that's already safely stored in your memory.

One of the easiest associations to utilize

is what I call the "Same Name Strategy." Everyone we meet is made up of thousands of characteristics. This is the combination that makes each person unique. But people also share many characteristics. You know lots of people who have the same body build, certain mannerisms or patterns of speech, or similar jobs and hobbies. That's a critical part of the ability to remember names. When you meet a new person you're looking for something that allows you to associate the new person with somebody of the same name whom you already know. Whatever the association is becomes the thread that will allow you to instantly weave the new person into your memory. Don't try to force bizarre associations, just go with whatever comes to mind.

Let's say you're introduced to a young lady named Ashley. You note that she is thin, with short-cropped hair, dark eyes, a bright smile, and very expressive facial features. These are some of the same characteristics that I've noted in the actress Ashley Judd. The link between the Ashley I just met and the Ashley I already know makes the association complete and instantaneous. In my mind, I'm going to the alignment of my brain cells that have already formed Ashley Judd in my mind to borrow some of that information to create the image of the new Ashley.

There's a very important aspect to this association business that you need to remember: Keep it simple! Use the least number of common characteristics you need to make the association. In my Ashley example, her name and haircut were sufficient. The other information is just supplementary, unless I find I have forgotten her name in the review process. Then, and only then, do I use her smile, her facial expressions, or other characteristics to strengthen the original connection. This supplemental information becomes strands that are woven around the original thread to strengthen the net.

It's just another example of how extraordinarily efficient your brain is and how little information it needs to "get it."

Sometimes there's a more efficient way than the Same Name Strategy to remember a name. That's usually true for someone who has an unusual name, like Khandi or, one of my favorites, Tomorrow Hughes. A name like that stands out so boldly that it doesn't require any association. That's the Von Restorff effect in action.

Okay, so the name of this person you're meeting now isn't unusual and your mental database isn't serving up someone with the same name with which to make associations. No problem! You still want to use your brain's ability to draw on existing patterns. Don't waste time building something when you can borrow what already exists. Your "people train" needs to switch tracks and go to another area to get it.

Recently, I met someone named Graham Spalding. His last name stood out because I wondered if he might be related to the Spalding sporting goods company. It so happens that one of my great pleasures in life is a good round of golf, and Spalding makes golf clubs and balls. But I made a common mistake. I was thinking about a previous conversation when I was introduced to Graham Spalding and missed his first name. Fortunately, someone else addressed him as Graham, so now I had the first name. I just needed to store it in my memory. I shifted mental tracks to search any other database I might have that contained the word *graham.* This is akin to how an Internet browser works. The first *graham* that popped up on my mental screen was the kind of cracker that my grandfather used to eat. I can see him sitting at the table with a stack of graham crackers beside a glass of milk. Applying the Law of Association, I envisioned Mr. Spalding chomping away on a graham cracker and the picture was complete.

Of course, if you don't know what a graham cracker is, my example doesn't work for you. They're still available on grocery-store shelves, but they aren't widely advertised and younger consumers mightn't have heard of them. So don't let my example force you into the same pattern. Run your mental train along other tracks looking for something to associate with Mr. Spalding's first name.

That search would fall into the category of what I call the No Prior Knowledge Strategy. We can use a partial pattern to complete the structure. It so happens that Mr. Spalding has neatly parted gray hair. The color of his hair sounds similar to the first syllable of his name. Gray. Graham. The sound is the key, not the image. If it is a double-syllable name, you double your chances for making a connection.

Then there's the Last Name Strategy. In today's more informal culture, we are likely to use a person's first name more often than the last name. As result, our database of first names may be a lot bigger than our database of surnames. Yet, there are situations in which protocol requires us to address someone as Mr. Smith or Ms. Jones, so we need to know how to remember last names as well as first names. Fortunately, the basic principles of learning first names apply to last names.

Start by becoming familiar with a wide range of surnames. The following list contains the ten most-common surnames of people in the United States, according to the 1990 census. You may also want to list your friends and other people within your circle of influence. Also look at *The People's Almanac* and make lists of surnames such as Aniston, Berry, Kidman, Cruz, Connery, and so on. You will find that the listing of the last name has a similar effect to that of reviewing the first name.

Smith	Davis
Johnson	Miller
Williams	Wilson
Jones	Moore
Brown	Taylor

If a name is unusual or stands out for some reason, then the problem is simplified as the Von Restorff effect comes into play. You can augment the Von Restorff effect by using parts of the name that are familiar to build your neural net. For example, if someone's last name is Patterson, watch that person's body language to see if he or she tends to pat a foot or a hand. Always be searching for similar brain patterns to make your connections.

If you aren't sure whether to use a person's first or last name, courtesy demands that you concentrate on the last name. That way, you can say, "Ms. Alexander, it is very nice to meet you," while waiting to see if she responds by asking you to call her Barbara. This gives you the advantage of hearing the first name twice to help seal it into your memory.

Then there's the First and Last Name Together Strategy. But be careful! This one is more difficult than you might think. That's because we tend to absorb the first name and the last name as two separate bits of information, then we try to store them simultaneously, the mental equivalent of multitasking. In chapter 8 we will discuss how trying to do too many things at once divides brain resources, creates inefficiency and stress, and can short-circuit the memory process. Besides, add too much information to the now-fragile neural nets and they tend to want to break apart.

The most efficient solution is to take the names together, not as separate bits but as one long multisyllabic word, like jennifer-anniston, halleberry, and tomcruise. This process, known as "chunking," helps you to see the image as one picture and hear the image as one sound.

For me, one of the challenges with this method is that I have always learned people by their first and then their last names, or vice versa. I have to unlearn what I have always done. The incorrect original learning is difficult to overcome. I also tend to focus on one name or the other. Graham Spalding, for example, has a last name that I found very easy to visualize, but it took a little more work to capture his first name.

The value of chunking together multisyllabic bits of information lies in its efficiency. You may remember that extraordinarily long word that was the title of a song in the musical *Mary Poppins*: "Supercalifragilisticexpialidocious." It's much easier to visualize Julie Andrews dancing with the children than to try to break down the word into fourteen monosyllabic words or images.

I must confess at this point that I don't do a lot of chunking. Rather, I choose to learn the first name and last name sequentially, starting with whichever name seems to be more prominent, and then linking the two together by a single image, just as I did with Graham Spalding. It's a bit more time consuming, but I'm able to allocate all of my mental resources to the task by focusing on strengthening the connection rather than risking information overload.

Reviewing for Retention

Now I'm going to save you lots of time. People seem to think they need to do a lot of reviewing and rehearsing to solidly capture a person's name. There's even a school of thought that requires you to use the person's name as often as possible. "Nice to meet you, Sara. How long have you been here, Sara? Why are you looking at me like that, Sara? Are you feeling well, Sara? Are you running from me, Sara?"

Nonsense!

Memory is a three-step process — reception, retention, and recall. Suppose you go to a social gathering for the first time. If the group receives you very well, chances are very high that you will be invited back again. So it is with memory. It is the strength of the reception that increases the probability of recall.

Notice that I didn't say "guaranteed recall," because there are three other factors — time, attention, and the number of people you are trying to remember. Time is the ultimate memory eraser, but only if it has something to erase. In my encounter with Mr. Spalding, my attention was drawn to his last name and my mind discarded his first name. I wasn't focused. I believe that's why most of us have trouble remembering names. We simply aren't focusing!

Another reason we may not be able to remember someone's name is that we weren't listening. Why? To be brutally honest, because we were too busy thinking about what we were going to say back to them. I find that if I can maintain a servant's mindset by thinking something like "What can I do for you?" whenever I meet someone, it removes the focus from me to thee and almost instantaneously mutes my internal voice so that I can really listen to the other person.

Finally, maintain eye contact for an appropriate length of time. You certainly don't want to scare anyone with a trancelike stare, but neither do you want to shift your eyes away too quickly. I've noticed that most people who feel they are poor with names also have poor eye contact during the initial seconds of the meeting.

Recall from chapter 5, "The Art and Science of Repetition," that time erases memories and that it does it rather quickly. To counter the deleting process, there needs to be a review of the name. The question is, how much review? The answer: it depends. Sorry, I don't mean to give such a dubious answer, but it's true. Sometimes, the visual connection and association you make with a person you're meeting for the first time is so strong that you need only a single repetition of the name to never forget it. For example, "Wow, I went to school with a Sara Bell and you could pass for her sister."

Of course, we seldom have the luxury of running into someone with the exact same name as someone from our past. So here's a process that I use, which you can adapt as you see fit to help you remember names.

I make a decision beforehand to remember the first, last, or both names of a person to whom I'm introduced. I'm often in large groups and it's easier for me to remember first names. In smaller, more intimate settings I'll try for both first and last names. If the group I'm in contains several married couples, I'll focus on last names, cutting the number of names I need to remember in half.

Upon being introduced to a person, I repeat the entire name once immediately after hearing it. You know that lack of attention isn't a factor at that moment because you're naturally focusing on the person. But don't be fooled into thinking you have the person's name stored after hearing it once. The retrieval of new information almost always takes longer than the initial reception, usually about three times longer. It will take several seconds for your brain to process this new information.

After anywhere from fifteen to thirty seconds have passed, repeat the person's name back to yourself. If you find you can't recall it, you're still early enough in the getting-to-know-you process that you can politely ask for a repetition of the name. If you were successful in repeating it the first time, do it again about thirty seconds later. If you can repeat the name twice, your learning period for that name is over.

But committing the name to your memory *isn't* over. Recall the forgetting curve in chapter 5 that shows us that we can forget up to 40 percent of new information in just twenty minutes. Time wants to erase that new memory from your brain. Because names are relatively arbitrary they are very time sensitive. You may pick any point along that forgetting curve, but for me, I choose somewhere around five minutes for a review session. I call it my "3 x 5 Rule" (3 times within 5 minutes). That should be sufficient for you to retain the person's name until the end of the day and, usually, for twenty-four hours or so. If I want to retain the name longer than that, then I will go back to the review frequency discussed in chapter 5.

You may find, to your pleasant surprise, that you are able to retain not only one but upward of three to four names using this same time frame. For example, you may be sequentially introduced to Joshua, Andrew, Emily, and Hannah. As you take time to say each name back to them, only about five to ten seconds have passed. The secret is to buy yourself a few more seconds by asking a question of one of the people you've just met, including his or her name in your question. But beware! If you're introduced to anyone else during this time frame, your mental hard drive becomes overloaded and may begin to crash.

Psychologists have concluded that we can retain about five to nine bits of information at any one time, with seven being about the average. They say that's why our phone numbers are seven digits long. When someone audibly gives out his or her phone number, there is more at work than just seven random digits; there is also a rhythm and a pattern. Assuming that the person is within your area code, he or she gives you three digits followed by a pause, then the remaining four digits. When you receive that information, you arrange it in the same pattern: 231-7896. People use patterns to recite and remember other numbers, as well, including Social Security numbers — i.e., the first three numbers, followed by a pause, the next two numbers and another pause, then the final four numbers. It seemed to take me forever to remember my daughter's Social Security number because she never paused in the right places. She gave me the first four, then paused, then the next three, then paused, then the last two.

Because names can be rather elusive, it is best to be conservative and to try not to max out your memory with five or more at any one time. The best way to discover how many people you can comfortably meet at any one time is to try these tests:

First, watch the first two or three minutes of a television show that you don't normally view. Pay attention to the names of the actors as they are shown on the screen, but only if they're shown at the same time the actor's face is shown. See how many you are able to recall at the first commercial break. You'll probably find that the names and faces are shown too quickly, so in the beginning just try to remember the first one or two names. If you do well in your commercial-break review, up the ante next time and call them by both their characters' names and their own names.

Next, if you are watching a show such as *Law and Order* or *CSI* with different characters each week, pay attention to the names of the guest characters as they introduce themselves. Say their names out loud as if you are repeating them back to them and then do it again after that fifteen- to thirty-second interval. Then try again after five minutes. You may find that you need to shorten the time. That's fine.

Now, watch a news channel when it is broadcasting national and international news. Pay attention to the names of the correspondents. The anchor usually introduces each correspondent and his or her name usually is shown on the screen. The correspondents usually wind up their reports by restating their names. That doesn't exactly conform to my 3 x 5 Rule, but you are being exposed to the name three times within a relatively short time frame.

As long as you've got the television on, tune to The Weather Channel just after *Local on the 8s.* Once again, the anchors are very good at introducing themselves. Their names also show up on a graphic for a few seconds after they return from a commercial break. The advantage (or disadvantage) is that you are being introduced to two people at the same time. This simultaneous processing of separate bits of information will be a good gauge as to whether you can chunk things together easily or if you are better at learning things sequentially.

Take a break from television and turn your attention to the daily newspaper, particularly to the local business section that showcases executive promotions and new hires. Also pay attention to any insurance or real estate ads that show several agents together. Do you notice a difference in your ability to remember depending on whether the photographs are in color or in black-and-white?

While you're browsing through the newspaper read the movie reviews of the latest releases. Pay special attention to who stars in each film and see if you can recall their faces just by looking at the names. Then try to recall some of the other movies you may have seen them in.

Finally, let's do some live practice. The next time you visit a grocery or hardware store in which clerks wear name tags, use the strategies we laid out early in this chapter to put some names with faces. Continue your shopping, then stroll through the store again in about five minutes to see if you are able to recall the names. This is great, noninvasive practice and you don't have to worry about hurting someone's feelings if you forget a name.

Use your next visit to a restaurant or a bank to pay special attention to the name of your server or your teller. Thank them for their service by name. This helps establish good practice habits of calling someone by name.

Recalling Names in Large Groups

Although I warned you earlier not to take on more than five names at a time, we all eventually find ourselves trapped in some work or social function in which dozens of people are milling around, many of whom we don't know. Don't panic! Remembering the names of a lot of people in a single setting is a matter of taking the small-group strategy and repeating it many times. There is an advertisement from a nationwide bank that says they don't process a billion checks a year without error, they process one check perfectly, then repeat that process a billion times. So it is with processing lots of names and faces.

Given unlimited time, we could, in theory, remember an unlimited number of people. But in practice it doesn't work that way. We are limited by time and thus there is a limit on the number of people we can remember. What is that upper limit? If you could remember the first names of one hundred people in about fifteen minutes, you might win a medal in the World Memory Championships, and you would certainly finish at or very near the top in the United States. Doing the math, that equals about six people a minute.

Practice with the 6 PPM (people per minute) goal in mind. Use some of the practice strategies we just went through to obtain lots of names, then apply this formula:

1. Repeat the small-group strategy for the second set of names. By the time you complete this, you will have eight people in your short-term memory who are in the process of being moved to your long-term memory.
2. Stop. Repeat to yourself the name of every person you have met up to this point, but repeat it in the reverse order. If you are successful, continue with the next set of four people. If you are unsuccessful, pause, relax, and repeat the names again in the order that you met them.
3. Repeat the small-group strategy until you have up to a maximum of sixteen people in your working memory. Learning the names of sixteen people in just five minutes is a tough job. If possible, try not to learn anyone else's name until about ten minutes or so have passed. Otherwise, the dreaded

information overload may crash your hard drive and force out everyone's name you have just learned.

Getting the Upper Hand

What we've been discussing up to this point are the core strategies for remembering names. By themselves these techniques will enable you to achieve impressive levels of recall. But there are some additional steps you can take, both before and after you meet new people, to reinforce the basic strategies. Let's start with some things you can do before you arrive at a social or work-related function to prepare yourself to meet new people.

The first step is to align your brain cells in a name-recalling mode. Get out your lists of most-popular first names and most common surnames and scan them for a few minutes before you leave the house. This will "prime" your brain for remembering new names once you arrive at the party or dinner.

If you're feeling really ambitious and have a corporate or industry function to attend, you can impress the group immensely if you show up knowing the names of everyone scheduled to attend, along with some knowledge about what they do, where they're from, and what position they hold. A few days before the meeting or conference is to convene, ask the planner for a detailed list of prospective attendees, including their positions. Usually the list will be in alphabetical order, a big help in memorizing it.

Next, using the Roman Room technique, set aside several rooms in your mind for this task. If there are going to be thirty people attending, then imagine three rooms. If you are familiar with some of the people, but not all, don't include the ones with whom you're familiar. As you review the list, place each person in sequential order around the room. If the first person on the list is Tom Apple, imagine someone you already know named Tom in position 1. If the next person on the list is Sara Bell, see a Sara whom you already know in position 2. It doesn't matter that you are not encoding their last names because the point of this exercise is to establish familiarity. The moment you meet Tom Apple for the first time, the Law of Association has already been at work and you can quickly link characteristics of the new Tom with the Tom you already know. The last names and other details about them will automatically fall into place as you get better at this exercise.

If you have additional information about them, you can add that as part of your mental image. If Sara is a manager for the electronics division, imagine the Sara you know working on a calculator, or whatever image comes to your mind first when you see her job title.

You will be able to assimilate names and faces very quickly using this technique. You also will know who was and who wasn't on the original list. This is always a great conversation starter: "Oh, Bill, I didn't see your name on the list. Is this your first time here?"

This method instills "value added" right away because the other person intuitively knows that you are prepared. Also, you are adding more people to your name database and it makes them easier to remember at the end of the day when you write about them in your journal. Your intelligence and organizational skills are subtly but impressively made using this technique.

You will also be better prepared to start networking. If you know a person's position, you already have some idea of what he or she does and you can have some questions, thoughts, or ideas prepared long before you meet.

When you leave the function, don't think it's over. You still have some memory work to do. If you didn't collect business cards from people you met at the conference, write their names in your journal. Briefly describe where you met them and, if possible, one or two facts about them. I find that when I review my journal years later, the faces come almost instantly to mind.

Next, practice the Rule of Ones with the people whom you meet. Be sure to review each name at the beginning of the next day, a week later, at the start of the next month, and before the end of the quarter. It takes just a few moments to do, but the rewards of increasing your memory, especially for names and faces, will benefit you many times over.

The Student Body

Educators can use a modification of this technique at the beginning of each new school year. First, get a list of the students' names before they ever arrive in your class. Educators, probably more than people in any other profession, have an extensive mental library of names and faces. Have the students sit in alphabetical order for the first few days. Review the list at home after the first day. Indicate on the list which names do not come to mind right away. This will often aid your memory the next time you see them, because we tend to remember better those whom we forgot the first time. You will find that your ability to assimilate names increases by orders of magnitude.

Emergency Name Recall

What do you do when you cannot remember someone's name who is approaching you or, worse, standing right in front of you? Here's my solution:

First, don't panic. We will discuss the devastating power of excessive stress in chapter 8. Do recognize and welcome, however, a small amount of stress. Being on what I call "alert status" is good because it helps us focus, somewhat like that first cup of coffee in the morning. Allow the heightened sense of tension to work for you by understanding that your mind is already beginning to search the databank for the name. When you're on alert status, you are also subconsciously perceiving and picking up nonverbal clues that you might not otherwise notice. You'll often find that as the person comes within talking distance, the name will appear in your mind. That happens because the mind looks for environmental clues to trigger a memory. That's why the Roman Room method is so successful: the environment never changes. When the person approaches, your brain is re-creating the environment from the last time you spoke with him or her.

Okay, let's assume that this time the name didn't just appear. Don't worry. Relax and focus on the conversation or make some kind of joke as the person approaches. Although some small amounts of stress can be good, a relaxed state is much more conducive to recall. Smile. A lot. Do you recall where you last saw this person? That can often jog loose the name. If not, ask him how his job is going or some other question that might elicit information that will trigger your memory.

Still nothing? Mentally review the alphabet quickly, but do it only once. Your brain is already in high gear and has probably already done this on a subconscious level. Your conscious review of the alphabet will draw your mind to the correct letter, and that, in turn, will release the name.

Finally, refocus on something else completely. I know, that's like my telling you not to think about the color red. It isn't easy. But if you can remove your mind from the name search, the name will often pop up. That's because your subconscious is trying to give you clues, but you've been so focused on trying to remember that you may not have been able to interpret the signals it is sending. How many times have you been driving down the road or doing something completely different when the name finally comes to you?

It helps, of course, if the person whose name you're trying to remember is part of a group. Sometimes other people will say the name you're trying to remember in the course of conversation. "Susan said something about that very thing yesterday." Susan! That's it!

Prepare yourself for these sorts of encounters by committing the forty most-popular names — twenty men and twenty women — according to the "Top 100" given to memory using the Roman Room method. Keep men and women in separate rooms, arranging them not by popularity but alphabetically. This helps with order

Top Ten Baby Names

If you have access to the Internet, go to www.ssa.gov and click on the most-popular-baby-name section for your year of birth. They have listed the top one thousand names for any year after 1879. The accompanying list shows the top ten baby names in 1963, the year I was born.

Male	Characteristics	Female	Characteristics
Michael		Lisa	
John		Mary	
David		Susan	
James		Karen	
Robert		Linda	

Mark	Donna
William	Patricia
Richard	Lori
Thomas	Sandra
Jeffrey	Cynthia

and speed as you are mentally reviewing the list while the person is standing in front of you. Sometimes, we may forget someone because the name is relatively common and the brain, oftentimes, is searching for the unique and novel. This task is much easier than you might imagine because you know, by now, that it is relatively simple to remember ten items after one or two reviews. It is easy to put familiar faces in familiar places.

Trust me, it takes much longer to tell you how to remember names than it will take you to learn to remember them.

Chapter Eight
Memory Enemies

Not surprisingly, my wife often is asked what it's like to live with someone who remembers everything.

"I wouldn't know," is her standard response.

And it's true, I forget lots of things. But as I've studied memory and how it works, I've become fascinated, not discouraged, by the things I don't remember. Instead of berating myself for forgetting something, I'll ask instead, "Why did I forget that?" The passage of time is, of course, one reason. But there are three other factors that I find play havoc with memory: stress, lack of sleep, and not paying attention.

Stress Kills

Time may be the number one enemy of memory, but at least it's gentle. It quietly erases things, almost unnoticed. Stress, on the other hand, is a brutal enemy of memory. It kills. Literally. Too much stress can damage regions of the brain, destroying cells. It blocks reception, inhibits retention, and chokes recall. It changes brain structure and function. Stress suppresses the birth of new neurons and shrinks existing ones. Worse, research is showing that lasting effects of stress can lead to other long-term effects on the body.

In April 2003, after attending a memory seminar in Florida, I was flying back home to North Carolina and had to pass through the inevitable Delta hub in Atlanta (there's an old saying that you can't even go to hell without flying through Atlanta). Security was at a high level. I had to show my driver's license at several checkpoints on the way to the gate area. Finally I passed through the last checkpoint. As I was walking down the corridor, the scent of sizzling hot dogs reminded me that I was hungry, so I got in line for a seven-dollar hot dog and a Diet Coke. When I opened up my wallet to pay, I saw that my driver's license was missing. I didn't panic immediately. I just assumed I had put it in another pocket after the last security check. But no, it wasn't in any other pocket.

Then I started to get worried. I must

have dropped it in the corridor, I thought. I hurriedly retraced my steps, but I didn't find the license. I went to the last security checkpoint I'd crossed and asked the uniformed guard if he had my license. Nope. And no one had turned it in at the lost-and-found desk.

My driver's license had just evaporated! I paced up and down that corridor with a rising sense of panic. Without my license, I couldn't get home. It was the only picture identification I had and I needed to show it to the boarding agent as I got onto the airplane. I had about an hour to find it before the boarding started. I kept checking back with the lost-and-found desk, to no avail. The airport made several announcements, but there was no response. I couldn't even rent a car to drive home. I was frustrated, angry, and panicked. Just before the last boarding call, I sat down, said a prayer, and meditated, trying to remove the overwhelming feelings of doom and dread.

Feeling more at peace, I made one last walk through the corridor and noticed for the first time a trash can that had been there all along. Suddenly I recalled that as I passed down the corridor the first time I had reached in my back pocket to toss away a rental car map. Had the license been thrown away with the map? Ignoring the odd stares from the passing throng, I began digging through the trash. Sure enough, lying on the very bottom of the can, under discarded hot dog wrappers, coffee cups, and layers of newspapers, was my license.

Why does this happen? I've described memory at the microscopic level as a chemical process that aligns neurons into specific patterns. Metaphorically speaking, I envision the process as the formation of neural nets that capture memories. Stress creates holes and tears in the net, which allow some experiences to slip right through. Researchers are more exacting. Studies have shown that when we are under extreme stress, we release an excessive amount of hormones that can interfere and block the chemistry of neural connections. The unraveling of the connections begins as the dendrites begin to shrivel, atrophy, and retract as a result of exposure to the excessive hormone levels. Additional studies reported in *The New England Journal of Medicine* suggest that chronic stress lasting for many months or years can kill neurons.

Some researchers are suggesting that stress may have a bigger effect on specific parts of the brain critical for memory, including the hippocampus. Excessive release of stress hormones can cause that part of the brain to atrophy. This seahorse-shaped structure plays a major role in consolidating working memory into long-term memory. Damage to the hippocampus can prevent the long-term storage of memories. Patients who have had severe damage to the hippocampus, or have had it removed, can remember things before the operation but not afterward. Events and experiences that happen today won't be remembered tomorrow.

The good news is that once stress is relieved, some components of the brain begin to repair themselves, growing new connections. Sometimes memories that seemed lost can return. In my Atlanta airport adventure, the specific memory of throwing away the map did not return to me until after the stress was relieved.

Because stress can interrupt the memory process, and even moderate chronic stress can damage the brain, it is important to develop personal strategies to reduce or overcome this insidious life force. Meditation works for me. In fact, meditation has become part of my regular routine because it helps take the worry out of the day. Of course, like other cancer victims, I've had some big worries in my life. But what I found really vexing was worrying about meeting someone in the grocery store or at the mall whose name I wouldn't be able to remember. Living with that kind of worry just seemed to make it worse. There are so many things in my life that I can't control, and to be completely honest, I don't always do well with the things that I can control. The Serenity Prayer is often a great comfort for me:

> God, grant me the serenity to accept
> the things I cannot change;
> Courage to change the things I can;
> And wisdom to know the difference.

Avoid stress! I try to stay out of stressful situations by doing my best to plan ahead and make wise choices. On big things like national television appearances, I always ask what I will be tested on. As long as I know in advance, I'm okay. Surprises, most of the time, end up being counterproductive. To avoid potentially embarrassing situations where I might not be able to recall someone's name instantly, I ask for a copy of the guest list in advance.

You can prepare for what may be

stressful situations by trying to re-create the environment as closely as possible. A team of Massachusetts Institute of Technology graduate students formed a company, bankrolled by $1 million, to gamble using card-counting techniques and memory skills. They practiced blackjack strategies until they knew them by heart. But they also knew that suspicious pit bosses, distracting waitresses, and hurried dealers diffused focus and added stress to the mental game. Team members spent time practicing under the same kinds of conditions they would encounter in the actual casinos, because it would take months to recover from a single mistake. The venture, recounted in the book *Bringing Down the House: The Inside Story of Six M.I.T. Students Who Took Vegas for Millions*, was wildly successful at least in part because of the players' ability to think and remember amid the pressure of the casinos.

Research studies show that the more one practices within the same kind of environment, the less become the effects of stress. For example, the more you do public speaking, the more comfortable you become, and your body does not secrete stress-related hormones.

You can substantially reduce stress by

staying within your limits. I know, the word *limit* can have negative connotations. It implies some kind of barrier that shouldn't be crossed. Break the speed limit and you risk a ticket. Overextend your credit limit and you risk the embarrassment of being "denied" at the cashier. A limit, however, can also afford protection. I know how quickly I can remember a deck of cards in front of the cameras or how many names and faces I can remember in a live audience within a given time frame. As long as I stay within my limits and try not to remember too much too quickly, stress isn't a factor. Only when I overextend myself do I begin to feel anxious and stressed. During one of the national memory tournaments, my goal was to remember one hundred words in perfect order within fifteen minutes. I had done it in practice several times. It was an attainable goal. But during the event I could see that my closest competitor was turning pages at a pace that indicated he was trying to remember more than one hundred words. I panicked and pushed harder, trying to match his attempt. It was a disaster for me. I blanked out on several words and scored a modest 79 out of a possible 100. Fortunately, my ambitious competitor overreached even worse. He scored 78 and I won the championship, but I could feel the lingering stress for the remaining three events.

You might also try to refocus on another environment. If you're waiting to deliver a speech or make a presentation to an important client, stress can develop in seconds, often just before you're due to take the stage. In that situation, physical exercise to relieve the stress is out of the question. What would your client's secretary think if you suddenly stood up and started doing deep knee bends? That's when I think of something completely different from the task at hand. Usually I try to redirect the rising stress by mentally playing a round of golf. I envision my favorite golf course and every detail that I can imagine, including the height of the grass, the tee location, where I want the ball to land, and the feel of the club in my hands. I even see the brand name and number on the golf ball. I add as much color and movement to the scene as possible. I focus on objective facts such as the gorgeous green of the grass, the sparkling white of the ball contrasting with the black of the letters, the shape of the fairway, the contour of the green, and the height of the flag. These facts are indisputable and prohibit subjective feelings from entering my mind. I don't try to replace my anxiety with artificial feelings of peace and serenity.

Your mind can have one thought at a time, while your body can experience many emotions simultaneously. When I feel myself about to be overwhelmed, I make sure that I have done everything that I could to prepare for the moment. If I failed to do something, I use that revelation as a point of thanksgiving, knowing that I will not repeat my mistake again. If nothing comes to mind, I try to suppress the emotions with the fact that I have done my best. Most of the time, trying to outthink the emotion works.

Sleep

People are always asking me about a "memory pill," something that you can get that is almost guaranteed to improve your memory.

I tell them to get a good night's sleep. A focused memory is a cognitive process requiring concentration, quick thinking, and creativity. Lack of sleep impairs these factors and can significantly degrade your working memory.

In 2001, after winning the National Memory Championships the first time, I was scheduled to appear on *Good Morning America* for an interview with Charlie Gibson, the genial host of that show. I was so excited at the prospect that I slept only fitfully the night before. When Janet and I arrived at the studio the next morning, the producers and crew made us feel very welcome. I wasn't stressed, but I did feel a little groggy. True to form, Charlie Gibson made me feel very relaxed during the interview. His questions were inquisitive but gentle. Then he shuffled half a deck of cards and gave me three minutes during a commercial break to remember the twenty-six cards. Three minutes to remember twenty-six cards is a breeze.

As I made a pass with each card, I could clearly see it in my mind and place it around the room, just as I have done hundreds of times before. There was no problem in the learning or encoding phase of the demonstration. However, because I was given ample time, I was able to make successive passes through the cards. With each pass, I noticed that the recall process was slower than normal. When the show came back from commercial, I began the recitation and I drew a blank on the fourth card, then the fifth card. This had never happened before! Stress began to build immediately. Indeed, I instinctively reached out and put my hand on Gibson's arm, probably a subconscious effort to brace myself in case I passed out there on national television. Thankfully, I remained conscious and somehow managed to remember the rest of the deck.

That panic-induced shot of adrenaline probably woke me up and helped me through that brief crisis. But there's no question in my mind that the lack of sleep the night before interfered with my recall process. I had trouble accessing the information. The pictures formed very slowly in my mind. It was as if my brain's neurons were groggy just like I was. This is very different from the effects of stress. Stress is like Teflon, keeping the information from sticking to my mental clipboard in the first place. Stress stops the memory process, while a lack of sleep slows it down.

A lack of sleep also interferes with the memory process because it dampens positive emotions. I notice that a poor night's sleep usually leaves me irritable, grumpy, and short-tempered. Emotions can become muted or simply absent. We know that emotions and memories are linked, and if emotions are affected or dampened, memory formation can be dampened as well. During the *Good Morning America* episode, sitting in the Green Room overlooking Times Square, most of the excitement that had kept me awake all night seemed to be drained from me. I was strangely emotionless.

According to researchers, there is a good physical reason for getting several hours of sleep. Dr. J. Allan Hobson, professor of psychiatry at Harvard Medical School, says that in order to be awake and aware, the brain needs two chemicals: noradrenaline and serotonin. According to Hobson, there is a specific part of the brain that is responsible for maintaining and releasing these chemicals, which in turn stimulate neurons all over the brain to help establish neural nets. In periods of concentration and focus, such as during a conversation, these chemicals are highly active, facilitating brain-cell-pattern formation and thus enabling memory. The minute attention is lost, the levels of serotonin and noradrenaline start to fall. The brain needs sleep to help regenerate these parts of the brain that release the chemicals. This is a process that apparently occurs only during REM, or rapid eye movement, sleep. Sleep is a recurring cycle with each cycle lasting 90 to 110 minutes and is divided into two categories: non-REM and REM sleep. REM sleep usually occurs about 70 minutes after we fall asleep. It is during this stage that most dreaming occurs. It is also during this stage that the cells and brain systems responsible for the production of serotonin and noradrenaline experience "downtime" and use this period to regenerate their transmitters. After REM sleep, the whole sleep cycle process begins again. This allows us to experience about five stages of REM per night.

On the eve of the *Good Morning America* appearance, I woke constantly, almost certainly disrupting my much-needed REM sleep. The chemicals that I needed to be alert were in low supply, making it more difficult than usual for me to form neural nets. After the commercial break, when I handed the cards back to the host, there were a few moments during which I was distracted as the crew turned off prompts and other visual aids to ensure that I couldn't see the cards Gibson was holding. That brief diversion of my attention may have caused my already depleted supply of brain chemicals to fall even further, something akin to the aftershocks that follow an earthquake. All told, the disaster was earthshaking to me.

The most common indication to me that I haven't gotten enough sleep is difficulty in the retention of names and faces. Remembering names arguably is one of the most demanding and difficult memory tasks. It requires an aura of relaxation, interest, association, focus, quick and creative thinking, expansion of working memory, and access to long-term memory. This is especially true when I'm trying to remember names in a large group of people. I was invited to speak to a group of fourth-graders to show them how they can improve their memory and study habits. The night before my appearance, the teacher called me to tell me how excited the kids were at my impending visit. They had been reading about me in the local newspaper and studying my story as part of their North Carolina knowledge. The teacher, doubtless to be supportive, told me that the kids were more excited about my visit than they had been when Senator Elizabeth Dole came to their classroom. Big mistake to tell me that!

"More excited than for Elizabeth Dole?" I repeated.

I appreciated the sentiment, but now I

was back in the same situation I was in the night before my *Good Morning America* appearance. I couldn't sleep that night, and the next morning I had that same groggy feeling that had preceded my *Good Morning America* near-debacle. Fearing a repeat performance, I decided I wouldn't try to remember a deck of cards for the fourth-graders. Instead, I would simply remember their names. Thankfully, I didn't tell them that I was going to do this; because as we went around the room with each child proudly telling me his or her name, I realized, to my growing horror, that the names were slipping right through my neural nets. Although stress became an increasing factor as the names continued, it was my lack of sleep the night before that had slowed my mental processes, making concentration nearly impossible.

If either stress or a lack of sleep alone can damage or slow your memory, just imagine what a potent memory weapon a sustained combination of the two can be. The trouble is, stress is often accompanied by a lack of sleep. If you're under stress and not sleeping because of it, you've got a powerful block to every aspect of your mental well-being, not just your memory. I've included some ideas for stress reduction in the accompanying sidebar. Experiment a little and find out which ones work best for you.

Lack of Attention

Watching television may be the world's most popular pastime. Some studies report that, on average, individuals in the industrialized world devote three hours a day to television, more time than they devote to anything else except work and sleep. What I find amazing about television is how much information we ingest while watching our favorite shows. When a program ends you probably can recite almost everything that happened from beginning to end, including specific lines and scenes. If you're really into it, you can even describe the clothes the actors were wearing and the cars they were driving. This is an extraordinary amount of detail.

The truth is, television is uniquely suited for focusing our attention. First, a television program gives us a sensory experience, filled with sight, sound, and movement. It becomes a multidimensional experience. It's also fast paced. Situations develop and are resolved quickly. And, of course, it's entertaining. There is humor or drama involved that touches one or more emotions and helps to engage us.

Beyond that, however, television programs are inherently interesting. We may find in a program a specific value — learning about a person or place through a documentary — or simply find that the program refocuses us from the stress of the day we're finishing. Because a television program is above all else visual, it mimics the way we think and remember. Unlike the actors, producers, and camera technicians, we don't see the written script that guides the production. Instead, we see pictures and scenes that touch off our instinctive reaction to sudden and novel stimulus. Finally, a television program is full of breaks. On commercially sponsored television, the breaks for commercials are obvious, usually painfully so. Programs on cable usually contain scenes in which the pace of the action slows briefly. We're not constantly bombarded by information, but receive it in easily consumable doses. We can mentally recap what has happened to that point.

You've doubtless noticed that when you're watching your favorite show, a question from your spouse or kids, the ringing of the telephone, or a knock at the door becomes an annoying distraction. You almost have to wrench yourself away from the invisible grip — might we say "addiction"? — of the screen.

We often betray our degree of interest in a subject by the way we look at it. Certainly if you pull your gaze away from the television set to check on your spouse or kids, you'll find them staring at the screen with an intense focus. A few years ago I was invited onto *The John Walsh Show* and told that I would be tested by having to remember the names of everyone in the studio audience. The producer gave me a microphone and about twenty minutes to commit to memory the hundred or so guests in the audience. As each person introduced himself or herself to me, the studio was otherwise silent. Indeed, the silence was rather distracting. As I looked up, almost everyone in the audience had their eyes intently focused on me.

I laughed. "You all are being so very quiet, but you should really see the way you are looking at me."

The man in front of me responded, "You should see the way you are looking at me."

It took me just a second to realize what he was saying. I stepped back and looked at the entire audience and asked, "Does it feel like I'm psychoanalyzing you?"

"Yes," they responded in unison.

There is another important facet of attention that you need to know about. Attention works best when it's focused on a single subject. We're all busy with a lot on our minds and a lot of responsibilities. It's gotten worse in the past several years as companies heap more and more work on fewer and fewer people, pretending that it's a simple matter of "work smarter, not harder."

Sorry, boss, that doesn't cut it.

That phrase is usually just a euphemism for multitasking, which leads to short-term memory impairment. Research studies show that trying to solve problems simultaneously instead of sequentially drastically cuts the brain's resources. Neural activity decreases when neurons juggle two tasks at once as compared with focusing on one task alone. Scientists say that such mental channel surfing can lead to a condition called "pseudo-attention deficit disorder." Psychiatrists Edward Hallowell and John Ratey, both of Harvard, find that people afflicted with pseudo-ADD have inadvertently trained their brains to constantly seek new information rather than thoroughly process existing information. As a result, they have difficulties concentrating and completing any single task well. Even if you don't suffer from pseudo-ADD, you may still have lost the ability to focus on the present because you allow your mind to be easily distracted. The information you're supposed to be gathering at the moment never gets into your mind because other, seemingly more important, matters are distracting you. Note the ticker at the bottom of the screen on a news channel. Is your attention divided as you listen and watch the screen while reading crawling text? If you find yourself distracted, you are probably dividing your mental resources.

I've found some techniques that are helpful in keeping my attention focused where it needs to be. First, recognize that your mind can hold only one thought at a time. It may seem that you're being bombarded by many things at once, but all that is happening is that your mind is shifting very rapidly from one subject to the next. You can overcome this rapid-fire switching by practicing holding on to a thought by asking questions to engage the thought or information. Ask what, how, who, when, why, and where. This helps construct a

Easy Does It: Stress Reduction Techniques That Work

1. Get into the habit of taking a walk and focus on new things you have never noticed before.
2. Go somewhere you have never been, such as a shop, a park, or a new café.
3. Go to a music store and listen to samples of the new CDs on the market.
4. Spend time in the art section of the library browsing through some of the magnificent books that depict the work of the great masters.
5. Build a collection of soothing music CDs and listen to them on a regular basis. You don't want to associate such music with times of stress and worry, so listen to them when you are happy as well.
6. Become involved with a small group such as a spiritual study group or five or six people who share similar interests and goals. Often the people who are the closest to you can help put things in the right perspective.

healthy mental environment that keeps un-related information from intruding.

You need also to recognize that there are always competing stimuli to distract you from your original thinking. Our brains are geared for what psychologists call an "ori-enting response." It's the way we normally react to a sudden new visual or auditory stimulus. You can use that natural wiring to help you visualize the information and amplify the sound of the speaker's voice.

We don't have a steady stream of new in-formation flowing into our brains. Instead, it comes in waves with pauses in between, all depending on how busy our day is. Use the "downtime" between new waves of in-formation to reflect on the last batch you received rather than to find some new task to fill the slack. Perhaps you can use the time to write down questions, or maybe to begin to develop a plan for how you are going to use the information to improve your work or your personal life.

As you already know, there's tremendous value in writing down things. Try a variant of your journal by writing not those things you want to remember but those things that you found most intrusive during the course of your day. You'll find that you begin to recognize these intrusions when they occur and can mentally push them aside, leaving your mind clear for the more important task at hand.

The big lesson of this chapter is to learn to recognize your memory's enemies, and then to defeat them. As I said earlier, we don't all cope with stress, sleep patterns, and attention spans in the same way. What's important is that you find what works best for you. Devising personal strategies to address each of these problems will lead to better mental health, a better memory, and a more positive view of life in general.

Chapter Nine
An Amazing Discovery

You've probably guessed by now that I like to watch television. Some of my favorite programs are on The Discovery Channel. That particular channel explores all sorts of interesting topics in ways that are very effective for me, since I can apply my memory methods, including SEA to See and the Law of Association, to remember much of what I've seen. But as much as I admired and enjoyed The Discovery Channel's offerings, it had never occurred to me that I one day might be the subject of one of those programs. Thus, the call I got on Friday, November 21, 2003, came as a total shock. The voice message was from Matt Meltzer, a producer for The Discovery Channel, who was working on a new show called *More Than Human.* One of the production teams researching memory on the Internet had come across my name. Matt wanted to know if I would be interested in being on the show to test some of my abilities.

Matt's message didn't say what kinds of tests they wanted to perform. Frankly, over the years I've learned to take a cautious approach to anyone who wants to test my memory. Memory, for all its strength and power, can be paradoxically fragile. Add a little pressure, mix in a little stress, combine it with an expectant audience, and you have a recipe for disaster. This is especially true if the information you are trying to process isn't familiar. Processing this kind of material takes longer, but television is unforgiving with time. Five seconds of "dead air" is an eternity on television. You might understand my trepidation when I returned Matt's phone call to see exactly what he had in mind.

I was relieved that Matt was very knowledgeable about the memory competitions in which I had been participating for the past few years. He said that much of what they wanted to do on the program was simply film some of those same skills.

I told Matt that my first reaction upon hearing his message was that he might be looking for someone who belonged in a Ripley's Believe It or Not museum.

Matt paused for a second. "Actually, some of the people who help produce the show used to work for Ripley's," he told me. But he quickly reassured me that the show he wanted to put together wasn't about human oddities or freaks.

"Our whole basis for producing programs for The Discovery Channel is to understand the reason and the science behind what seem to be incredible feats," he said. "We have a team of researchers who carefully analyze the abilities of the people who we bring on the show. Each researcher develops an area of expertise to explain a feat in a way that the viewer can see why it's possible." He mentioned as an example a show in production that involved a man who could catch an arrow in midflight. The show would use high-speed photography to literally capture the moment. Other sophisticated instruments would be used to measure the man's reflexes. The show would compare these extraordinary reflexes with those of the program's host, John Pullum, to illustrate the vast difference between the arrow catcher's amazingly fast responses and those of an ordinary person.

Then Matt told me that in my case, the producers were already talking to researchers at Wake Forest Medical Center about possible ways of peering inside my brain to see what was happening as I memorized information. He said they would use Functional Magnetic Resonance Imaging to get motion pictures of the electrical activity in my brain compared to that activity in someone whose memory wasn't trained.

Without knowing it, of course, the producers of this Discovery Channel program were bringing one of the most terrifying experiences in my life full circle. I told you earlier how our daughter, Kristen, had lapsed into a coma as a result of a viral infection in her brain. At one point, her memory centers were so severely affected that she didn't recognize her mother or me. Even though she was fully awake and alert, she seemed to regard us with the suspicion due complete strangers. Kristen is now living a healthy and normal life with no side effects from this infection, due in large part to the expertise, treatment, and care she received at Wake Forest Medical Center. Suddenly I had the chance to give back to the research experts at the medical center and learn something about myself at the same time. Of course I would do the show!

Filming the Brain

Three weeks later, as we were waiting for the camera crew to set up all their equipment in the library at the Wake Forest Medical Center, I was introduced to the researchers from the Advanced Neuroscience Imaging Research Lab. They would run the segment in the show that took a movie of my brain while I memorized information. Dr. Joseph Maldjian led the team, which included Dr. Paul Laurienti, whom you met earlier in this book, as well as Dr. Bob Kraft, an assistant professor of medical engineering, and Dr. Jonathan Burdette, also an assistant professor of biomedical engineering.

Young, bright, and enthusiastic, the team was as curious about me as I was about them. The difference was in the amount of faith we had in one another. Because of our family's history with Wake Forest, I had tremendous faith in their abilities and expertise. They, however, had only recently heard about me and were clearly a little skeptical of the value of this experiment. Their skepticism probably was reinforced when a respected staff member who wasn't on the research team inquired about all the commotion. Told that The Discovery Channel was about to film a man who could remember a deck of cards after one sighting and remember hundreds of numbers in just a few minutes, he scoffed. "No one can do that kind of thing," he said as he walked away.

The tests that the producers and researchers had devised were familiar to me and particularly suited to making this study of memory visually appealing. The first test was for me to remember a shuffled deck of cards. The host of the show, John Pullum, warned me before we sat down in front of the cameras that "I'm really interested in watching you do this because when I first heard about this particular 'memory feat,' I thought you might be manipulating the cards in some way. I'm a professional magician and, as you can imagine, I'm pretty adept with cards."

To prove his point, he shuffled through the deck of cards we were going to use, put it on the table, and then asked me to name my favorite card. I didn't really have a favorite, so I just chose the jack of clubs. He turned over the top card. It was the jack of clubs! It was my turn to be amazed. I don't know how he did it, but he made his point.

When the lights came on he reshuffled the cards, gave them to me, and watched me like a hawk. Although I was focused on the task, his intense focus on my hands was almost distracting. But I passed the test.

"The concern I had was that you had previously memorized a deck of cards and were using sleight of hand to reorganize the deck I shuffled to match up with the deck you had previously remembered," Pullum told me. "Obviously, that wasn't the case. I'm impressed. Scott Hagwood, you are more than human."

I didn't realize that the cameras were still rolling. The producers used Pullum's last statement on the air, resulting in innumerable jokes and heckling from family and friends ever since. I can't tell you how many times someone has said to me, "Scott, surely you can remember this because, after all, you're more than human."

The second test involved committing to memory a 160-digit random number with only five minutes of study time. When it came time to repeat the number, I was told to look at Pullum, who had the number hidden inside an envelope. The number was loaded into a computer that allowed the producers to project the number on the television screens of viewers, although

I, of course, couldn't see it. As I recited each digit, it was shown on the screen. As I neared the end of the 160-digit number, I heard expressions of amazement from the research team, who hadn't seen the first test in which I remembered the deck of cards. As soon as we took a break, Dr. Laurienti came up to me. "Scott, we knew you had some kind of system to be able to remember numbers, but to see this in real life is truly amazing."

I was a bit surprised that they were so surprised. After all, these guys were top researchers, experts in how the brain functions. If they were amazed by the ability of an ordinary human being to use his memory effectively, how much greater would the skepticism be among the general public? That's when I realized that I would have to prove myself over and over again, in every situation, in every speech or workshop I conducted. People want — no, they *need* — to see it being done. The message and the messenger are inseparable.

I'm a Believer?

The next test produced an interesting — and unscripted — result. Fifty random words had been written on cue cards and I was to remember all the words in the specific order that I had seen them. The words were both concrete and abstract: potato, yield, satisfy, guard, etc. First, the host showed both me and the television audience the cue cards, one at a time. Then the cue cards were shown only to the camera, not to me, as I recalled each word in order. As I recited each word, the host showed the card to the audience, then tossed it aside. When the test was over — I performed perfectly — there was a heap of cue cards on the floor. Nobody seemed to care and we all went off to get coffee and prepare for the next round of taping.

About an hour later, when we returned to the room, the cue cards were still in a jumbled mess on the floor. As one of the crew members leaned over to begin picking them up, I casually remarked that "potato" was the thirty-first card that I had seen. "I wondered how it had wound up on top."

For a moment, there was silence in the room. Then Tony Vigaro, the director of the show, asked, "Scott, can you sort through these cue cards and put them back in the original order that you called them out?"

I told him I didn't see why not. Just to make sure that the cue cards were in random order, members of the crew got down on the floor and reshuffled them. Tony instructed that all the cameras be turned on and then put a timer on me to see how quickly it would take. In about three minutes, I had put together the cards in their original order. That unscripted feat became part of the premiere of *More Than Human* in January 2004.

Still, there remained a tiny element of doubt even among the crew, all of whom now knew my ordinary background and had seen me use my memory as they taped for twelve hours. As we were preparing to leave the taping room, Tony Vigaro turned to me. "Scott, is this really something I can do?"

This is what makes talking and writing about memory so challenging. Even people experienced in the field of memory, and people who have seen a lot of unusual things, approach their own abilities with some degree of doubt. That is why it is so important that you work through the exercises in this book. That's the only way you can convince yourself that you have the ability to remember almost anything.

Changing Your Brain

A more important reason to do these exercises is that the strategies and techniques I'm telling you about change not only your perception of how you think, they actually change your brain to make thinking and remembering easier and more efficient. Using Functional Magnetic Resonance Imaging (fMRI) technology, the research team at Wake Forest Medical Center proved this with my own brain.

This technology has been used in thousands of studies to explore different areas of brain activation, including face and word recognition, working memory, false memories, anticipation of pain, and the struggle to make tough decisions. Dr. David Cox of the Massachusetts Institute of Technology has found that volunteers looking at different objects produce brain patterns on an fMRI that are so distinctive that he could examine a series of fMRI films and correctly determine which object the person was viewing when the scan was made.

Now, as we approached the part of the lab that had been reserved for my scan, Dr. Maldjian explained how the machine works. An fMRI machine uses a large magnet to induce radio signals from the chemicals in the brain. Different chemicals produce different frequencies. A quiet brain overall produces a frequency that shows on the fMRI machine as a red area. When a region in the brain is activated and blood surges into that area, the frequency changes, producing a yellow color on the fMRI monitor. The increase in blood flow corresponds to increased neuronal activity, which indicates an increase in the firing of individual neurons. The parts of the brain that are activated during a thinking or memory task show up in color and in cross-sectional images that can then be re-assembled in a 3-D image on a computer screen. This allows researchers to rotate the image to see which areas are responsible for memory. They can also see the intensity of the areas of the brain responsible for recall by the change in colors.

My test would take about an hour, during which I needed to remain very still. I wondered how I could do that while flipping through a deck of cards. "Don't worry," he said, "you'll be equipped with special goggles that allow you to see cards on a computer screen." I would respond by clicking on a mouse situated near my left knee. A left click would mean Yes, and a right click No. Thus I was able to move my hands without moving my head.

The tests the good doctors had devised were tough. During one test I was shown cards at a rate of one every two seconds. That was much faster than I thought I could retain. After looking at the series of cards, there would be a thirty-second delay before I was shown a second series of cards. The task was to determine the exact sequence of the cards I had seen. For example, if the first card they showed me in the second series was an ace of diamonds, I had to remember if the first card in the original series was indeed the ace of diamonds.

The test was unbelievably difficult. At some points during the recall, they might show me the queen of diamonds when I knew the queen of hearts was supposed to be the next card. It took a moment to see the difference, make the determination, click the mouse, then prepare for the next card on the screen. That's a lot to do in only two seconds. My brain felt as if it were on fire.

What I didn't know at the time was that Dr. Burdette had taken the same test the day before, acting as a control subject,

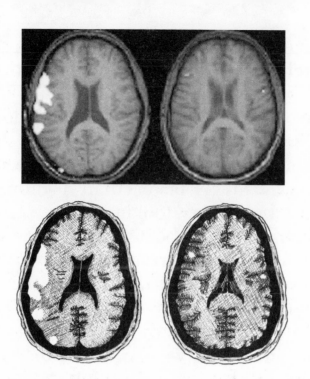

The image on the left is the control subject, where the areas of activation are seen by the glowing regions. My brain image is on the right, showing only one small region of activation. (Scan results courtesy of Wake Forest University School of Medicine, Advanced Neuroscience Imaging Research Lab. Drawing courtesy of David K. Childers.)

which would allow the team to compare two brains doing the same task. When my scan was complete we went to review the films of my scan and Dr. Burdette's. I couldn't believe it! I expected my brain scan to show swirling patterns of red changing to yellow and back again as I struggled to remember which cards in the second series were the same as those in the first. Yet, all I saw was the accompanying picture. One small area was glowing yellow. Dr. Burdette's brain, though, was indeed a beehive of glowing activity, as you can see on page 234, where there is a black-and-white reproduction of the photo. (To view a color version, visit my web site at www.scotthagwood.com.) The other tests were even more difficult, but the results were just as dramatic. "They made my head hurt," Dr. Burdette said of the exercises.

Now, Dr. Burdette is no dummy. On the contrary, he's a lot smarter than I am. But in the final analysis, I was using a small fraction of my brain compared to his. The results, Dr. Maldjian said, were "pretty unbelievable. Scott was performing well above the ninety-ninth percentile and once you get there, you are just off the charts." Both he and Dr. Laurienti attributed these results not to any special genetic predisposition but to the way that I had trained my brain to make it highly efficient. The brain is remarkable. It needs to use only a fraction of its capacity to achieve extraordinary results. The exercises that I performed for the scan and that I undertake in memory contests often involve cards, names, or words. But it isn't *what* you're memorizing that's important, it's *how* you're memorizing. You want your brain to master the *process* of memorizing. That's where it gains the immense efficiencies. Once you have the process down pat, you can remember anything.

A trained brain is more efficient at least in part because it is able to eliminate confusion. While the brain appears to be highly compartmentalized — that is, vision, sound, smell, etc., are located in different parts of the organ — most stimuli activate different parts of the brain to some extent. However, a highly trained brain uses just enough resources from other compartments to amplify any signal, but not so much that it causes interference or wastes energy. The control subject's brain is a model of confusion and wasted energy. Obviously, there's lots of activity, but nothing is getting accomplished. This untrained brain, shown on the left, was uncertain how to process the tasks and tried to solve the problem using different approaches simultaneously. The brain shown on the right is highly organized and knew exactly where to process the incoming stream of information.

Dr. Burdette's brain scan illustrates the problem of internal competition. One reason he didn't perform well is that the brain was activating all its resources simultaneously, igniting internal competition between the various compartments that were literally competing to process the same information. While each part of the brain alone is remarkably effective at its job, the overall effect was that no one section took command of the problem. The trained brain, on the other hand, used only the minimum resources necessary to accomplish the task. The expertise of the other compartments was vital to the success of the highly trained area, but they were used only as much as was needed and no more than that.

The memory exercises in this book not only improve your mental health but make your mind amazingly more efficient. You can do more using less. The well-trained brain is the ultimate model of efficiency. If only everything else were as efficient. Just imagine the immense increases in efficiency that any company that could harness these effects among its employees would enjoy. Everyone would truly "work smarter, not harder." But don't wait for your employer to set up a memory-training program. Do it yourself now and capture that incredible power to make your life more efficient and more fun.

Chapter Ten
Putting Your Memory to Work

There's no question about it, a developed memory will enhance your social life. People like others to be interested in them and know about them. With an enhanced memory you will find yourself a charming and skilled listener, someone always welcome at a party or other social gathering. But it's in the workplace that your memory will make a huge difference. A developed memory is the mother of every transferable skill in the workplace. It encompasses every major category you need to succeed, both professionally and personally. Memory is a process. Master your memory and you have mastered the process and all the skills and abilities it takes to become extraordinary.

Transferable Skills

Research involves the abilities to observe, investigate, study, perceive, sense, measure, test, inspect, and examine. Developing your memory increases your observation skills. You become more aware of your surroundings and you naturally attune yourself to detail. You also investigate what works well and what does not. When you write to remember, you are asking the kinds of questions at the end of the day that allow you to understand how you naturally receive and record information. Your study skills increase dramatically because you become better able to focus your attention. You understand the learning process and how to minimize repetitions. Developing your memory increases your perception because you become adept at drawing from your long-term memory. You become more sensitive to both external and internal clues. Your senses become heightened because you have developed a natural strength to encode new information.

Analysis involves activities that encourage us to compare, extract, correlate, derive, evaluate, differentiate, and identify.

This is truly your memory at work. If we held everything in our mind, then we would not have the power of choice because everything would have equal weight. We train our memories to retain the value and discard the debris.

Interpretation is the ability to explain, understand, portray, and advise. A developed memory changes the way that we think, and we actually begin to see the world from a different perspective. We internalize information by converting it to images and experiences that make sense to us and allow us to combine it with our previous knowledge. When this information is pooled with the accumulation of other experiences in our long-term memory, we have more resources from which to draw to help explain and interpret the world around us.

Here's a list of other transferable skills. Sure, go ahead and memorize them as part of your memory exercises. But also think about whether each one can be served by a more powerful memory. I think you'll be impressed by what you discover.

problem solving	planning
leadership	follow-through
innovation	vision

synthesis	sympathy
negotiation	flexibility
team player	installing
systematizing	management
decision making	mentoring
imagination	listening
artistry	empathy
initiative	presentation
assembly	operating

Everyday Uses for Extraordinary Memories

The first time I heard of the National Memory Championships was by chance. Late one February evening in 2000, I was channel surfing and came across a young lady reciting "the eight of hearts, the jack of spades, the queen of diamonds . . ." It took me a minute to figure out that she was reciting a partial deck of cards. ABC's *20/20* was doing a feature on a very unusual competition being held in New York and the woman, Tatiana Cooley, had just won the National Memory Championships for the third consecutive time. Tatiana, a twenty-eight-year-old advertising assistant, said she hadn't been born with an unusually good memory. Rather, she said, her ability was the result of a system she used that took just a little bit of practice to enable her to perform amazing feats. The show then switched to an interview with Tony Buzan, the author of the books that I had purchased to help with my memory. He was the co-chairman of the event. I went to the ABC Web site to find out more about the tournament and perhaps find a way to meet Tony. When I read more about how tough the particular tests in the memory competition were, I knew there was no hope I'd ever be a competitor. If I wanted to meet Tony, I'd have to be in the audience.

My assumption that I couldn't compete with the likes of Tatiana Cooley was significant. Up to that point I had read the books and even experienced some modest success at being able to remember a shuffled deck of playing cards. Yet, when I saw the level of competition and the specific requirements of each event, especially the time constraints, I fell from grace. No longer was I a disciple of memory. Suddenly I was a nonbeliever. I had no faith that I could do this. Nor did I have any inclination to try, because the contests seemed too overwhelming.

But then a strange thing happened. During the Thanksgiving holiday we went to visit my parents in Morristown, Tennessee, a little town of just over twenty thousand people. My brothers David and Bradley also came home for the weekend. During the annual family touch-football game, I badly twisted my ankle. That evening, laid up with a swollen ankle, I took some good-natured ribbing from Bradley about how I was getting old, fat, and slow.

"Well, I might have gained a few pounds," I retorted, "but I've also gotten smarter. I bet you I can remember a deck of cards in about ten minutes, and I won't even touch the deck. Go find a pack of cards, shuffle them, and call them out to me, one at a time, and when you get to the end, I bet I can repeat it."

Bradley looked skeptical, but he took the bet. When he finished calling them out to me, I immediately repeated them back to him in the proper order. It was almost worth the whole cancer-treatment process, the twisted ankle, and the hours of memory practice to see the stunned look on his face.

Then I told him about what I had learned about memory during the long hours of recovery, the tournament I had seen on TV earlier in the year, and the fact that the next one was coming up in May 2001. He asked me if I was going to enter the tournament.

"No way," I said. "You know how I bombed tests in school. I'm not going on national television to show the entire world what an idiot I am. Let's just reserve that little secret for you and me and the rest of the people in Morristown."

Bradley's response startled me. "Man, you've been through cancer, what could be worse? Besides, wouldn't it be cool to go up to New York and take a side trip to Atlantic City and make a few bucks off this new skill of yours?"

I told him I wasn't interested in making any enemies of tough guys in dark suits, but it got me to thinking. He was right. It couldn't be any worse than cancer. Besides, it might be a chance to exorcise some of the old exam demons that still haunted me from time to time. From that moment on, I began to give serious thought to entering the competition. Instead of my being anxious, there was a strange kind of peacefulness that accompanied the decision. Funny, if it hadn't been for the sprain, I probably wouldn't have had that conversation with Bradley. Other than Janet, I had never shown anyone the card skill I had developed, because that kind of thing just doesn't come up in regular conversation.

I didn't understand at first why there were so many events. Why not just one or two? Although it would take me months to believe the answer, I learned that the events were designed to test the strength of memory in many areas and to demonstrate that memory could be improved in all areas. If you are mastering the memory process, then it does not really matter what you are trying to remember. I also didn't understand at first that all these events had real-world applications. But as I began to practice, I discovered all kinds of hidden secrets that became the practice strategies I've revealed to you. Here's what each facet of the National Memory Championship tests is all about. (For a complete set of rules and how the events are scored, see the appendix, The Rules of the Memory Competition.)

Speed Cards

The goal in this event is to commit to memory and recall a single pack of fifty-two cards in the shortest time possible.

Contestants are given up to five minutes to remember as many cards as possible in order. This is torturous because most of us have difficulty remembering more than about seven bits of information before our memories crash. Distinguishing the difference between the 3 of hearts and the 3 of diamonds can be visually demanding because they have identical numbers and both are red. The top contestants need only a single sighting of each card and can review an entire deck in about a minute. For you inveterate card players, this is a great way to fine-tune your game, whether it's bridge, hearts, or spades. It's also a great mental exercise to develop as a baseline for your memory. If, for example, you know that you routinely can remember a deck of cards in about five minutes, you can use that to measure whether a bad night's sleep or unusual stress is adversely affecting your memory. A significantly longer time span than five minutes would be a warning that you're overtaxed.

Hour Cards

In this event the contestants commit to memory as many decks of cards as possible within an hour. The hard part about this is the sheer volume of information. To remember multiple decks of cards, you simply must learn to enhance your thinking process. This stretches the limits of your working memory as focus and mental organization become highly honed skills.

Spoken Numbers

Imagine someone reciting a list of random numbers at the rate of one per second. That's what happens in this event, and the challenge is to remember as many of those numbers — in the correct order — as possible. This event is tough because you hear the numbers only one time and they are given so quickly that your listening skills must be at an all-time high. Because the numbers are random, there is no way to predict what the next number will be, and so you have to suppress the brain's natural tendency to anticipate. When you listen to someone speak, your thought process is always ahead of the verbiage as your brain tries to anticipate what the speaker will say, so that it can make a judgment on whether or not the information is important enough to keep. Trying this a few times will make you more aware of the speed of your thought process, not to mention making it easier to remember phone numbers, tracking numbers, or order numbers if they're given to you verbally.

Historical and Future Dates

This competition requires the contestants to remember as many fictional, numerical historical and future dates as possible and link them to the corresponding fictional events. There are eighty "historic" dates. For example, a contestant may see this text: "In the year 2042, sailboats were banned from the Indian Ocean." Then, on the answer paper, the text would be given and the contestant would have to identify the correct year the boats were banned. Contestants have only five minutes to memorize the dates and events before matching them up. It's easy to get the dates and events mixed up unless you have a developed memory. This is a very practical skill, not only for students but for anyone who works with regulations, such as the lawyers, accountants, architects, and builders, since it helps eliminate or at least reduce the amount of time going back to the original books.

Sprint Numbers

The aim of this event is to remember as many random digits (1, 3, 2, 7, 9, etc.) as possible within five minutes. As if memorizing lots of random numbers in the correct sequence isn't tough enough, the scoring in this event is brutal! Contestants record sequences of forty numbers on each line of their answer sheets. One point is awarded for each number recalled correctly in sequence. A juxtaposition of two numbers counts as two mistakes, and any line with two mistakes isn't counted at all! It sounds arbitrarily mean-spirited, but there's a point to it. If you forget a single digit in a telephone number, the rest of the numbers are useless. If you juxtapose two numbers in a banking statement, the consequences could be disastrous. If you confuse probabilities and percentages in a presentation or speech you are making, your credibility flies out the window.

If you work with numbers, whether telephone numbers, financial statements, or credit cards, you'll appreciate the value of this exercise. Remember the game Concentration? It's the game in which cards are arranged in a grid pattern and you have to match the new card you've just looked at with a card that you've already seen. Mastering this game is a piece of cake because you have to see the card only once to remember. For example, let's say the grid had six rows and five columns. The card in the first column and first row would translate to the number eleven. The card in the first column and second row would translate to twelve. The card in the fifth column and sixth row would be fifty-six. Since you already have images associated with the numbers eleven, twelve, and all the way through fifty-six, you simply apply the Law of Association to link the picture on the cards to the row and column number.

Chemistry students can use this method to memorize the periodic table of elements quickly and easily. I wish I had known how to do this back when I was in school. It might have saved me from getting that six out of a possible one hundred points on that crucial chemistry exam. For example, the element in the first column (family) and the first row (period) of the table is hydrogen. My image for the number eleven is a professor friend of mine by the name of Tat who teaches at a local college. Hydrogen is a gas, much lighter than air, so I might see Tat, who is normally a well-grounded individual, floating around near the ceiling in his lecture hall. The next element in the first column and second row is lithium, an essential component in grease or paint. Since my image for twelve is Tawny Kitaen, of White Snake video fame, I might see her with greasy hair or hot pink painted nails or both.

No matter which numbers are used, you can use this method to remember them quickly. Oftentimes, someone will give me a phone number or an address over the cell phone when I am not in a position to write it down. But you might want to discover where and when you need the ability to remember numbers. As you write to remember, pay attention to the times during the day that you needed to have a number and it just wasn't there. The ability to remember numbers instantly is not only a great mental exercise, it is a subtle way to convey your intelligence.

As of this writing, the world record for number recall is 327 digits, which is greater than 1 digit per second and is held by Jan Formann of Denmark. A score of 120 digits in the United States competition will place in the top three. The average digits remembered for the U.S. event is approximately 40.

One-Hour Numbers

This is a variation on the Sprint Numbers exercise. In this event contestants are asked to memorize as many random digits (1, 3, 2, 7, 9, etc.) as possible within sixty minutes and recall them perfectly. The hardest part about this is the time factor. You are fighting the power of time's ability to erase information from your working memory. As of this writing, the world record for remembering numbers in open competition is 1,920 and is also held by Jan. If you do the math you'll see that Jan's pace for remembering random digits in the sprint contest is 1 per second, but in this contest it falls to one digit every two seconds. That's the result of the necessary review process to remember the vast amount of information taken in over an hour's time versus just five minutes.

Random Words

In this event contestants are asked to remember as many random words as possible — guilt, flower, walk, airplane, etc. — in order after fifteen minutes of memorization. The tough part about this event is converting abstract words into concrete images and learning to spell them correctly. For better or worse, the advent of spell check on computers has eroded my ability and desire to spell words correctly because I know the computer will catch my mistakes.

One of the great things about mastering this skill using the Roman Room method is that you will far exceed the norms for word recall. Research shows that a person given ten words and asked to repeat them in order will begin to falter at the sixth word and few make it past the eighth word. After just a few practice sessions, you will be in the 90 percent range.

Mental smugness aside, there may be times when you're in the middle of an informal conversation with a group of coworkers in which valuable business advice is being bantered around. It won't be the time or place to pull out a pencil and piece of paper. But you don't have to. You merely store the advice in your memory.

Let's create a hypothetical conversation around the lunch table.

"Boy, I've really found caller-ID is a great advantage. When I see who it is calling, I pull information of that account before I even pick up the phone. That impresses the hell out of whoever's calling."

"I've done something similar with my Palm Pilot. It has a cell phone in it and if I let it ring a few extra times, I can begin to pull up the data on the caller."

As the conversation continues along those lines, you can be picking out key words and, using the Roman Room technique, you can "see" in your mind the words *caller-ID, computer, relationship, Palm Pilot,* etc. Use the natural lag in conversation to mentally reinforce these items by applying the SEA to See method.

You might be interested in exploring the skill of speed reading. Speed reading involves learning to identify the main point, or central idea, on a page by training your brain to suppress everything else. Gleaning the key words into a mental list and using the Roman Room method to recall it will help accelerate your comprehension of the material.

And who among us hasn't had a brilliant idea while stuck in traffic or taking a shower? There are many times when pen and paper simply aren't handy. Mastering the skill of creating mental lists helps to capture ideas that would otherwise slip away through the flow of time or be blown away by the swirling winds of distraction.

The most effective use of this skill in the workplace is to help you master the art of verbal presentation. Cicero used it over two thousand years ago to express his vast knowledge of information without notes. So impressive were his performances that we will honor his name and contribution to public oratory by calling this method the Roman Room. Perhaps you want to make five points in a group discussion. But if people keep interrupting with questions or comments, it's easy to get distracted and lose your train of thought. Using the Roman Room method to place your ideas in very specific locations will always keep you on point and focused. You will find that you are able to encourage questions without the fear of forgetting to make any of your main points.

Finally, mastering this skill is mastering a beautiful way to enrich your life. If you are able to remember hundreds of random words, you are also able to remember hundreds of ideas in a very short time. You can learn to add value to your life while standing in line at the grocery store merely thumbing through magazines with valuable tips. I recall that a single edition of *Fortune* magazine contained articles about fifteen ways to boost income, three rules for finding the next Dell, five dream retirement towns, and three places to stash money for college. That was a profitable five-minute wait in the checkout line!

Names and Faces

The goal in this event is to commit to memory as many names as possible, then match them to the right faces. This event is a lot more difficult than meeting someone for the first time and remembering his or her name. That's because a photograph doesn't convey all the other information that results from a face-to-face meeting, such as the sound of the person's voice and any odd little mannerisms. But if you practice learning names this way — using newspaper and magazine ads or studying the names and faces of actors in an unfamiliar television show — you'll find that when you are meeting someone in person, your ability to learn the new name will be sharply improved. Because you have gotten by on so little information before, the presence of a person gives you an almost overwhelming amount of information.

This exercise is also good to help you learn the names of the people in your organization. You may use a pictorial directory or log on to the company Web site. On my first job I was sent to corporate headquarters. But before I left for the airport, my boss stopped me and gave me a group photograph of the corporate executives. He pointed to one gentleman and asked me if I knew who he was. I had no idea.

"That's the president of the company," he said. "You may run into him or some of the other people in this picture at lunch or in the hall somewhere. Here, take it. Learn their names."

I never asked why he took the time to seek me out and give me that photograph, but I suspect there was an embarrassing moment in his early days at the company that he didn't want me to repeat.

Studying pictures of people and putting the names to the faces also is very helpful if you are going to visit another company.

Not only does it make a tremendous impression, it's a valuable expression of the high level of service that you are willing to provide. Just one note of caution: People don't always look like their photographs; women's hair color changes, people gain or lose weight, they get older (and don't always want an up-to-date photo) or they may switch from glasses to contact lenses.

Learning names and faces is the hardest of memory tasks. Names are elusive, arbitrary, and abstract. Compared to this, you'll find the other exercises easy. But this is an important skill to master because it is transferable and can be used in other areas. You're also increasing your name database in what will become a perpetual expansion. The more names you can remember, the more names you are able to store in your long-term memory, making the process easier and easier.

Binary Numbers

I admit it, committing strings of binary numbers to memory may not be high on the list of things you want to accomplish in your life, but it is a very difficult mental task to remember random sequences of ones and zeros in perfect order. However, if you have mastered the ability to remember regular numbers, it is much easier to do. The secret is to convert the binary numbers to regular numbers, or, in other words, go from base 2 to base 10 numbers. The accompanying table converts binary to base 10.

So, if the binary number was 1 1 1 0 1 0, I would take the first three digits, seven, and the last three digits, two, and convert that to seventy-two.

Conversion—Binary to Base 10

Binary	Base 10
001	1
010	2
011	3
100	4
101	5
110	6
111	7

Poem

In this event contestants are asked to memorize an original, unpublished poem. The poem, composed for the contest, doesn't rhyme. The hardest part about this event is remembering the punctuation, including capitalization and italics. Learning to master this event is good for remembering scripture, code, or even your speeches, word for word. You can use the same strategy to remember song lyrics. Here's how I do it:

The first time I listen to the song, I get a feel for the rhythm and the pattern of the melody. Although up-tempo songs can be learned in this manner, it works very well for slower tunes.

Then I listen carefully to where the singer emphasizes words or specific phrases that highlight the meaning of the verse or the chorus and begin to visualize these. Since the chorus is usually repeated several times in the song, the second time I hear the chorus I begin to create a story in my mind using the imagery. I link the first major word or phrase in the chorus with the next major word or phrase by having the images interact with each other. This is identical to the blending technique that I discussed in the random-number method. For example, in the song from *The Wizard of Oz*, I see lemon drops melting on a chimney. This single image gives me the exact wording of the phrase because the small, supporting words or ideas naturally fall into place. I do not make an individual image for each word.

In an earlier exercise, I asked you to turn the book upside down and read a line or two. You discovered that the brain needs only a few clues to fill in the blanks. Use this natural ability and combine it with the art of visualization to accelerate your ability to learn songs, text, scripture, and poetry. For longer texts or scripts, use the Roman Room method. Visualize the central word or idea in the sentence or the phrase and then place it around the room, or rooms.

If you find that you are really interested in learning more text, consider learning sign language. Not only does it give you another language, but it is universal, visual, filled with movement, and easy to learn. You will also be able to communicate with people who would otherwise be outside your circle of influence.

As you now realize, developing your

memory not only increases your power by increasing your knowledge base, it enhances almost every ability you possess and every skill you want to develop. It accelerates learning, diffuses information overload, and creates multitudes of value in your life. Now that you're armed with the tools to do amazing things with your memory, you can become a grand master of memory by mastering these seven fundamentals of memory:

1. Your memory is virtually picture perfect. Learn to develop this natural ability.
2. Memory is an experience. Use your SEA of knowledge to transform images into multidimensional experiences.
3. Draw from what you know. We are an accumulation of life experiences, full of facts, figures, people, and millions of bits of information. Apply the Law of Association to accelerate your learning.
4. Use the Rule of Ones to minimize repetition, maximize time, and create great study habits. Benefit from your increased memory power.
5. Stress hurts. Develop personal strategies to help reduce its devastating power.

6. Sleep. Get a good night's rest. Do this every night.
7. Increase your attention span. Try not to let your mind be preoccupied by past events or your to-do list.

Find a "permanent storage" room in your home, and commit to memory these Seven Fundamentals of Memory:

1. Picture
2. Experience
3. Knowledge
4. Rule
5. Stress
6. Sleep
7. Attention

The next chapter lays out a week-long series of exercises, most of which you've already encountered in this book, that will demonstrate to you the immense power of your memory. I'm betting that if you do these exercises for one week they will leave you astounded at your abilities. If you like the results after that week, you can keep doing them at progressive levels of difficulty to create an even more powerful memory. Grab your workout gear and come with me to The Memory Gym.

Chapter Eleven
The Memory Gym

I hope that as you've read this book you've also tried some of the suggested exercises. If you have, I think you now have a good feel for how much you can improve your memory and, by improving your memory, improve your life. If you've already tried some of the exercises in the seven-day workout in this chapter, that will help reinforce your memory skills. If you haven't tried the exercises, prepare to be amazed! Seven days from day one, you won't believe how much more powerful your memory is.

Just because I've laid out a seven-day set of exercises doesn't mean you have to do one every day with no breaks in between. This isn't meant to be discipline, it's supposed to be fun. Skip a day or two or three if you need to. And, just like the real gyms with exercise bikes, StairMasters, and weights, some people will find they're addicted to memory workouts. If you become an addict, you can engage in these exercises at different levels of difficulty. I also urge you to go back and look at some of the exercises that aren't included here in the gym and give those a try, too.

Day One

Take half an hour after dinner to write a journal entry in which you recall significant events of the day, both the high points and the low points. Write briefly about people you met, decisions you made, and things you wish to remember. When your journal entry is finished, reread it and fill out an Element Box to identify which of the Three Reversible Laws of Engagement you used: your senses, emotions, and actions. Finally, read your journal entry again and summarize the major parts of it as single key words recorded in a Key Word table.

But wait — this particular workout isn't over yet. Tomorrow morning, as you start your day, perhaps over breakfast, go back to the Key Word Table you constructed the night before and see if each key word triggers a memory. If a word doesn't trigger a memory, go back to your journal entry to see what the word was supposed to remind you about. Key words and their ability to trigger memories are a foundation for the

Roman Room exercise that we'll come to shortly.

If you want to push yourself harder on this exercise, simply make a commitment to do it every day. At the end of a week, you'll go back to see how many of the key words you listed over the past seven days still trigger the intended memory.

Day Two

Pick up a book or a magazine and turn to a chapter or an article you've already read and enjoyed. Now turn the book or magazine upside down and read the chapter or article from beginning to end. You should find it getting easier and easier to do as you progress through the text. Your brain is adapting to make associations between what would otherwise be gibberish and words that you already know.

Next, using the same chapter or article, go through and choose two words at random. For this exercise, don't choose definite articles (*the, an*), prepositions (*of*), or conjunctions (*and*). Construct a sentence using those two words.

Finally, go back to the two random words you chose. Visualize each one, writing down what your mind's eye sees as representative of each word. Don't struggle. Take the first image that comes to mind with each word. Don't worry about *why* it came to mind, just accept it. When you've visualized both words separately, go back and visualize, using senses, emotions, and actions (SEA to See), what they look like *together.*

Day Three

Developing your memory is a bit of a paradox because you expand your ability to remember by forgetting. You've picked up this book for a reason. Perhaps you want to become better at retaining names and faces. Perhaps you want to enrich your life through memorizing lists. Whatever the reason, at some point during our time together, you have forgotten something. Today's exercise is about developing the attitude of fascination. As I've said earlier in this book, your ability to recall information is never in question. It's the process that needs to be honed. An unknown teacher of rhetoric in ancient Rome, circa 86–82 BC, compiled a text titled *Rhetorica ad Herennium* for students developing the art of memory. In it, the author says:

We ought, then, to set up images of a kind that can adhere longest in memory. And we shall do so if we establish similitudes as striking as possible; if we set up images that are not many or vague but active; if we assign to them exceptional beauty or singular ugliness; if we ornament some of them, as with crowns or purple cloaks, so that the similitude may be more distinct to us; or if we somehow disfigure them, as by introducing one stained with blood or soiled with mud or smeared with red paint, so that its form is more striking, or by assigning certain comic affects to our images, for that too, will ensure our remembering them more readily. The things we easily remember when they are real we likewise remember without difficulty when they are figments.

Figments are the focused images you are storing away in your long-term memory, like the painting of the five questions that you ask someone in order to get to know them better. You are imitating nature when you are developing your focused memory. That is why it is so important to understand what you remember naturally as you write to remember. However, when you forget, part of the art of memory is enhancing your forgotten figment by adding an additional element from your SEA of knowledge to the image to make it more striking. A second part of the art of memory is learning to give the image time to develop in your mind. When I mentioned the five questions above, did the image come right away or did it take a moment or two? You will find that as you develop your memory, the speed at which the images or information returns to your mental eye increases.

Why?

Because the gateway between your retention and your recall becomes a well-worn path. You begin to trust your impressions. You become more confident in your mental abilities. Today, review some of the things that you have set out to remember. Go back over some of the exercises in this book that have been interesting to you and see how many of the items you are able to remember. In the following days, I will give you a list of things to remember. But, as you review these lists, twenty-four hours later, a week later, whatever your time frame, learn to become fascinated when you forget, because that is the only way to establish a deeply trodden path between your long-term memory and your mental eye.

Day Four

I want to let you in on a little secret that is not so secret — numbers can be confusing. They are too random to remember. There is usually no sequence, pattern, or logic to a phone number, a license plate, a gym locker, or a credit card. But that's okay. Developing a great memory is about creating order out of chaos. Let me show you how the great memorizers of the world are able to remember hundreds and even thousands of numbers. There's nothing new about this, it's a technique that has been used for hundreds of years. In 1648, a man by the name of Winckelmann first introduced the concept of representing numerals with letters of the alphabet. One hundred and fifty years later, a fellow named Gregor von Feinaigle refined the method and lectured on this art throughout Europe. His numeric-alphabet code was published in 1813. The table on page 273 is a modification of the system to help you better visualize the letters with the numbers.

Here's a two-part exercise to help you master this method. First, take scrap pieces of paper or index cards and write the number on the front and the corresponding letter or sound on the back. Mix them up and when you see the numbers on the front, first visualize the letter before you say the sound. You will find that in a very short time you are able to see letters in the numbers.

The second part of the exercise is to convert numbers to images. Let's take the first numbers, 1 through 10. But let's modify the process a little by letting the number 1 be represented as 01, the number 2 as 02, and so on.

In the table on page 274, I will give you the first letter and end letter and you fill in the blank with an image. For example, look at the very first entry. My vision of the number 1 is John Travolta dancing in the white leisure suit from the movie that made him so famous. Apply the SEA to See to make the images multidimensional experiences.

Now that you have your images, repeat the index-card exercise, but this time, to the back, add the image you made. You will have to make a new card for the 10. Review the cards until you can successfully

Numeric-Alphabet Code

Number	Letter	Visualization/Auditory
1	T	Like the Roman numeral I for the number 1
2	N	Like the Roman numeral II for 2 but with a single downstroke
3	M	Like the Roman numeral III for 3 but with two downstrokes
4	R	It has the letter r at the end.
5	L	Similar to the Roman numeral for 50
6	d	Flip the letter d around and it looks like a 6.
7	K	Flip 7 around, add a downstroke, and it's similar to the letter k.
8	f	Write a lowercase f in cursive and it looks similar.
9	p	Flip 9 around and it looks like a p.
0	s	A coiled-up snake

Creating Multidimensional Images

Number	Word	Image
01	S T	Suit – John Travolta from *Saturday Night Fever*
02	S N	
03	S M	
04	S R	
05	S L	
06	S D	
07	S K	
08	S F	
09	S P	
10	T S	

recall each image twice. Then, as always, take a 15-minute break, come back, and see if you can repeat it without error. If you find this exercise fascinating, and feel so inclined, in subsequent days make a similar table for the numbers 11 through 20, then 21 through 30, and so on until you reach 99. If you make an image for the number 00 (mine is of Dr. Seuss or actually of the Cat in the Hat from one of his most famous books), you will have 100 images in your mind that represent every number you will ever need to know.

In the memory championships the number line may look something like this:

1 8 0 0 9 7 8 4 3 8 0 1 1 4 9 5 4 7 2 3

But I see it as pairs like this:

18–00 97–84 38–01 14–95 47–23

My images, correspondingly, are (look at the code above to see how I might have derived these images): taffy–Seuss–puck– fire–mafia–suit–tire–pill–rake–gnome.

I would simply take these ten images and place them inside the Roman Room. Thus, I am able to recall any of these numbers forward, backward, or in any other order, just like you have already done. You are creating order out of chaos. Although numbers are indeed random, you can pair any number with an image you have already created.

Day Five

Create a Roman Room using the room in your house or apartment in which you spend the most time. Begin with the corner located over your left shoulder when you enter the room. That will always be position 1. Follow the sequence corner–wall–corner–wall–corner–wall–corner–wall around the room from left to right. Thus, the wall to your left is position 2. The next corner is position 3, and so on. When you finish the corner–wall sequence you'll have 8 positions. Add the floor as position 9 and the ceiling as position 10 and you're set to do your first room.

Now look around the room in sequence again and visualize a single detail about whatever object occupies each position in a room, focusing on some small detail that will always bring the object into clear focus. It can be a vase of a certain color, a table of a certain wood, a lamp with a certain shade, a television with the manufacturer's trademark. If there is not an object in a certain position, look at the molding or the walls very carefully for small imperfections. Any detail is significant and will remain fixed in your mind. If no imperfection exists in that position, pick any random portable object in the house and temporarily place it there.

Next, dust the room with a cloth or brush, touching each object you identified above. You're interacting with the object and transforming it into an experience. Use windows, light switches, paintings, carpet — whatever happens to be there. Make a table similar to the accompanying one for the room.

Now take ten pieces of scrap paper and number them 1 through 10. Put the scraps in a hat and draw one. Let's say you draw the number 5. Start counting from position 1 (over your left shoulder when you entered the room) and move sequentially to position 5. That should be the corner in front of you to your right as you enter the room. Note the object in position 5. Repeat this exercise at least five times and you will begin to see how quickly your eyes and your mind adapt to the pattern. After a few more repetitions, it will become automatic. When you draw the number 10, your eyes will immediately go to the ceiling.

Charting a Room

Position	Location	Object
1	Corner	speaker
2	Wall	TV console
3	Corner	rocking chair
4	Wall	fireplace
5	Corner	recliner
6	Wall	doorway
7	Corner	lamp table
8	Wall	sleeper sofa
9	Floor	coffee table
10	Ceiling	ceiling fan

After you complete at least five repetitions of the number-drawing exercise, relax for ten to fifteen minutes or do something else completely off task: read, take a walk, work on a crossword puzzle, make a phone call, whatever. Then, wherever you are, close your eyes and re-create the room in your mind. Slowly count forward, 1 through 10, seeing each object in your mind, then count backward, again seeing each object until you reach 1. Repeat this mental process at least five times, each time speeding up the process.

Finally, make a list of things to remember. It can be a grocery list, a list of your favorite movies, or the names of ten coworkers. Remember, at this point it isn't *what* you're remembering, it's *how* you're remembering. If you want to make it easier, here's a list of the top ten songs of the twentieth century compiled by the Arts and Recording Industry of America:

1. Over the Rainbow — Judy Garland
2. White Christmas — Bing Crosby
3. This Land Is Your Land — Woody Guthrie
4. Respect — Aretha Franklin
5. American Pie — Don McLean
6. Boogie Woogie Bugle Boy — The Andrews Sisters
7. West Side Story (album) — the original Broadway cast
8. Take Me Out to the Ball Game — Billy Murray
9. You've Lost That Lovin' Feelin' — The Righteous Brothers
10. The Entertainer — Scott Joplin

If you're using the list of popular songs, condense each title into a single mental image accompanied, of course, by a few bars of the song, or use your mental picture of the artist as representative of the song. Starting at the top, put Judy Garland in the corner to your left, position 1. Bing goes on the wall to your left, position number 2. Continue to place all ten in order around the room, ending with The Righteous Brothers on the floor and Scott Joplin hanging from the ceiling. Now pull the scraps of paper with numbers out of the hat and see if you don't find Aretha Franklin looking at you across the room from position 4. If you're using your own list, simply generate a visualization of each item on your list and place it in the correct position around the room.

Congratulations, you've created your first Roman Room, the single most important step you can take on your way to a more powerful memory.

Day Six

Building on what you learned about the Roman Room in the preceding exercise, this time you'll construct three Roman Rooms, demonstrating the almost infinite availability of rooms in which you can park memories.

Imagine that you are touring your home or apartment with a guest. You begin at the front door and move about the various rooms. You do it in a very specific pattern that is logical, that flows with the layout of the floor. Physically do this with three rooms — you're welcome to use a bathroom or even a closet if your living quarters are small — to create three Roman Rooms. Be sure to use rooms you have not used in any other exercise. Using the method from the preceding exercise, the corner of the first room will be position 1 and the ceiling of that room will be 10, the corner of the next room you enter will be position 11, and the ceiling of that room will be 20. As you enter the third room, the first corner will be 21 and the ceiling will be 30. You now have thirty places that are being organized into your long-term memory. Physically review the rooms and places again. Then, mentally walk through each room, noting the places and objects you are committing to memory. Pay particular interest to the ceiling of the room you're leaving and the first object of the next room. Make sure that visual link is established so you can readily see it in your mind's eye. Then take thirty numbered scraps of paper, put them in a hat, and draw them one by one, in your mind going to the designated place in the three rooms. Do this five times, then take a break and do something else for at least fifteen minutes. Now count backward from 30, visiting each spot in each of the three rooms in reverse order. Once you can see each object or position in every room, twice, you are ready to take a giant leap in expanding your mental abilities.

To save you the time of compiling your own list of thirty things to remember, we'll use this exercise to learn the phonetic alphabet (you'll sound like an airline pilot if you do this out loud). The object is to create a visual object with each alphabetic word listed in the accompanying table and associate it with the corresponding object or position in each room. Remember, this is a Memory Gym. Instead of lifting weights to build physical strength, you are building mental strength. You are organizing your mind. You are developing your abilities in the areas of patterns, sequence, and logic. You are also cultivating your imagination, creativity, innovativeness, problem-solving, and synthesis skills. You are developing your unique memory process.

The Pilot's Alphabet

Number	Alphabet	Your Image
1	Alpha	
2	Bravo	
3	Charlie	
4	Delta	
5	Echo	
6	Foxtrot	
7	Golf	
8	Hotel	
9	India	
10	Juliet	
11	Kilo	
12	Lima	
13	Mike	
14	November	
15	Oscar	
16	Papa	
17	Quebec	
18	Romeo	
19	Sierra	

Number	Alphabet	Your Image
20	Tango	
21	Uniform	
22	Victor	
23	Whiskey	
24	X-ray	
25	Yankee	
26	Zulu	

Repeat each object in your mind once. Wait about a minute, then repeat them again, but this time do it backward. Now, go back to your hat. Begin to draw out numbers. What you are able to do is not only repeat the alphabet backward but know that the *L* is the twelfth letter of the alphabet and *S* is the nineteenth and so on. Successful completion of this exercise puts you well on your way to mental mastery. You really begin to understand that there are no limits to what you can remember and how you remember it. Amazing!

Day Seven

This final exercise is another two-parter. In the morning, using a list of the 100 Most Popular Names similar to the Social

Top Ten Baby Names in 1963

Male	Characteristics	Female	Characteristics
Michael		Lisa	
John		Mary	
David		Susan	
James		Karen	
Robert		Linda	
Mark		Donna	
William		Patricia	
Richard		Lori	
Thomas		Sandra	
Jeffrey		Cynthia	

Security Administration Web site mentioned on page 163, take ten male and ten female names and construct a table like the accompanying one. Look at each name on the list and see if you remember anyone with the same name. It needn't be a close acquaintance; it can be a movie star, a politician, an author, or friends from your elementary or high school days. Write down some characteristic you recall about each person you remember. During the course of the day look at the names two or three more times and add to the list any other people you recall with the same name. The point of this exercise is twofold: first, to show you how many people you really know, and, second, to get you accustomed to noticing characteristics that make people memorable to you.

The second half of this exercise takes place in the evening. First, watch the first two or three minutes of a television show that you don't normally view. Pay attention to the names of the actors as they are shown on the screen, but only if they're shown along with the actor's face. See how many you are able to recall at the first commercial break. You'll probably find that the names and faces are shown too quickly, so in the beginning try to remember just the first one or two names. If you do well in your commercial-break review, up the ante next time and call the actor by both the character's name and the actor's own name.

As long as you've got the television on, tune to The Weather Channel just after *Local on the 8s.* Once again, the anchors are very good at introducing themselves. Their names also show up on a graphic for a few seconds after they return from a commercial break. The advantage (or disadvantage) is that you are being introduced to two people at the same time. This simultaneous processing of separate bits of information will be a good gauge as to whether you can chunk things together easily or if you are better at learning things sequentially.

Take a break from watching television and turn your attention to the daily newspaper, particularly the local business section that showcases executive promotions and new hires. Also pay attention to any insurance or real estate ads that show several agents together. Do you notice a difference in your ability to remember depending on whether the photographs are in color or in black-and-white?

If you want to expand your ability to recall names, engage in some live practice. If you visit a grocery or hardware store in which clerks wear name tags, use the strategies we laid out in chapter 7 to put some names with faces. When you've finished shopping, stroll through the store again in about five minutes to see if you are able to recall the employees' names.

That's it. You now have the tools to continue to expand your memory for the rest of your life. There are no limits.

It's All in the Cards!

Here's a little bonus exercise for those of you who would like to surprise your friends and family with your new memory skills. It's something I use when I lecture on Memory Power.

You're already familiar with the number-alphabet system from the earlier exercises. That same idea is used to develop the ability to remember a completely shuffled deck of cards. Like *breakfast* and *vacation* — words that are turned into multidimensional experiences — cards are converted into moving images as well. For example, the 2 of clubs represents an image. For me it is one of those orange cones along the highway wherever road work is being done. How did I come up with cone? Because the suit is clubs, the object begins with *c*. Using the number-alphabet system, you know that "2" represents *n*. So, when I filled in the blank between c——n, the first image that came to me was an orange cone. Now, an object just kind of sits there. To make it an experience, you should associate someone you know, or a celebrity, doing something with it. In this case, I see Paul Newman idly twirling the cone, much as he might have done in the movie *Cool Hand Luke.* In a way, each card is a mental icon representing a miniexperience. For me, a deck of cards does not represent four suits of thirteen cards; it represents fifty-two miniexperiences. Each of them is unique. Even though the order of the cards changes each time they are shuffled, the miniexperience that you associate with them does not. Using the Roman Room method, you place each image along the room, just like you would with any list, and then recall it forward, backward, or in any other order.

When I filled in the blank between c——m, for the 3 of clubs, the first object that came to mind was a comb. Then, drawing from my SEA of knowledge, the first person who came to mind who might use a comb was the fictional character Rapunzel, who combs her long flowing auburn hair several times a day. These are simple but powerful images because they are familiar and they have movement.

For example, if I am reviewing a deck of cards, I prepare my mind by first mentally walking through six rooms in my home, as if I were giving a tour to someone. I stop in each room and identify the ten positions of each corner, wall, floor, and ceiling before moving on to the next room. This process occurs very quickly, usually less than a minute but no longer than two. Why six rooms? Each room will contain ten cards. Since there are fifty-two cards in a deck, I need two spaces in the sixth room.

As an example, let's use my living room, which you know so very well by now. If the first card in a shuffled deck happens to be the 2 of clubs, I see Paul Newman twirling the orange cone atop the speakers. If the next card is the 3 of clubs, I see Rapunzel combing her hair on the television. As I look at each card, I see the image. I put the image atop or within each position in every room, just like Cicero did nearly two thousand years ago. When I recall the deck of cards, I simply go into every room and "see" the image associated with each position. If someone asked me, "What is the second card you saw?" I would simply go to position 2 in my mind, which we know is the TV, and see the image of Rapunzel with her comb. It is, of course, the 3 of clubs.

This exercise develops your mind in extraordinary ways. First of all, you may not really believe it is possible for you to do this. I know I didn't. But let me ask you to try one suit today. It's only thirteen cards. You know by now that you can remember thirteen things relatively easily. I wish I'd had a mentor to help me do this when I got started, but I am going to save you many hours of trial-and-error practice. Second, you are applying the numeric alphabet in a fun way. This will help you to remember numbers for any situation. Third, you are creating order out of chaos. Fourth, you are becoming mentally fit by developing your imagination, improving your focus, increasing your concentration, fine-tuning your storytelling ability, and molding your brain to become highly efficient. Fifth, you are understanding how you learn, because you are getting a sense of how long it takes you to learn something

Establishing an Image

Card	Image	Celebrity
A♣	c——t	
2♣	c——n	
3♣	c——m	
4♣	c——r	
5♣	c——l	
6♣	c——d	
7♣	c——k	
8♣	c——f	
9♣	c——p	
10♣	c——s	
J♣		
Q♣		
K♣		

new and to know how long you want to re-member it using the Ebbinghaus forgetting curve and the Rule of Ones.

1. Review the numeric alphabet from Day Four.
2. On a table, deal out all the cards with clubs as if you were playing solitaire,

but order them from the ace of clubs, 2 of clubs, 3 of clubs, all the way through the king of clubs. The ace will be card 1.

3. Use the accompanying table to establish an image for each card. (Hint: For the jack, queen, and king, reserve those images for elegant people whom you might imagine doing something "at the club." The king may be the president, the queen the hostess, and the jack an important officer.)

4. Once the image has been established, imagine a celebrity doing something with it.

5. On the back of the cards, with an indelible-ink pen write the object/celebrity story.

6. Once you have the images with each card, review them backward while they are still lying on the table. Take as much time as you need to apply deliberate intensity to each image. Remember the rocket analogy?

7. Now, prepare to be amazed. Pick up the suit, shuffle the cards, and turn the pile up so that you can see the first card. Look at the random cards, one card at a time, and see if you can "see" the image in your mind. If you draw a

blank, simply look at the back of the card. This should be enough to help you remember the image the next time you go through it. If you repeatedly come up to that card and still draw a blank, return to your SEA of knowledge and add one and only one element to make the image more vivid.

8. Go through the thirteen cards of the suit until you can successfully repeat each card you have seen twice, without error. Take a fifteen-minute break, then repeat the exercise again.

This exercise is designed to help you become aware of the extraordinary power of your mind. You are converting cards to images, much like a musician converts notes, which are but scribbles on paper, to beautiful music. This marks the end of this day's exercise. If you want to explore this further, shuffle the thirteen cards again, and then place each image in the positions of two Roman Rooms. Feel free to review the cards as many times as it takes, associating each image with the objects, walls, corners, etc., in your two mental rooms. Then see if you are able to recall them backward, forward, or in any random order.

To remember an entire deck of cards, repeat the exercise with the remaining suits. Be sure, as you are creating an image, that the first letter of the image begins with the first letter of the suit. Thus, all images you create with the suit of diamonds begin with the letter *d*.

Now go amaze your family and friends and introduce them to the possibility that they, too, can have a powerful, life-enriching memory.

Appendix
The Rules of the Memory Competition

Event Title			Poem
Aim			To commit to memory and recall a poem.
Time to Memorize			15 minutes
Time to Recall			30 minutes
Question Paper			1. A previously unpublished poem (consisting of the title, lines of verse, and the poet's name) written specifically for the competition. (Sponsor's text can be substituted.) 2. Translations are available for the World Memory Championships but must be ordered at least eight weeks before the competition.
Answer Paper			1. Contestants must recall the poem from the beginning by writing it down exactly as it was written (the title and the author also score) on the lined paper provided. 2. Contestants must make it clear where one line ends and another line starts. 3. Contestants must make it clear where lines have been left out from their recall of the poem (two omitted lines maximum allowed).

Event Title	Poem (continued)

Scoring	1. Marks are awarded for correctly recalling:
	  a. Every correctly spelled word.
	  b. Every incidence of a capital letter.
	  c. Each punctuation mark (to include italics, underlining).
	2. Each line has a different number of points available, but to score those points, the line has to be perfect.
	3. In the World Memory Championships where several translations of the same poem are being used, each translation will be a line-by-line translation of the English version and so the points designated for the English version will be assigned to each translation on a corresponding line-by-line basis.
	4. The same evaluation of mistakes is applied as to that in all similar disciplines: i.e., one mistake in a line, then the line counts ½; two mistakes, the whole line is counted as 0 points.
	5. For the last line only: A partially completed final line of

Event Title	Poem (continued)
Scoring (continued)	the answer scores the marks for the portion remembered if the line is correct as far as it goes.
	6. *If a word/expression has been clearly memorized, i.e., *the main structure clearly resembles* the word to be memorized, but has been spelled in an incorrect way, no points are given for this word. It will not, however, cancel other words in a line. For example, if somebody writes "rythm" instead of "rhythm," no points will be given for this word, but, if all other words in the line are correct, full marks minus one will be given for that line.

*This rule has been introduced to limit the complications that may arise from spelling ambiguities, autographical mistakes in translations, dyslexia, and handicaps for foreigners, etc.

Event Title	Binary Numbers
Aim	To commit to memory as many binary digits (101101, etc.) as possible and recall them perfectly.
Time to Memorize	30 minutes
Time to Recall	60 minutes
Question Paper	1. Computer-generated numbers are presented in rows of 30 digits with 25 rows per page (750 digits per page).
	2. 4,500 digits (6 sheets) are presented, although more are available from the adjudicator but this must be requested one month in advance of the competition.
Answer Paper	1. Contestants must write their recalled numbers in rows of 30 digits.
	2. Contestants may use the answer sheets provided or their own (as long as it has been cleared by the adjudicator before recall commences).
	3. It must be clear how the rows presented on the answer paper relate to the rows on the question paper (missing rows must be clearly indicated).

Event Title	Binary Numbers (continued)
Scoring	1. 30 points are awarded for every complete row that is correctly recalled in order.
	2. For every complete row of 30 that has a single mistake in it (this includes a missing digit), 15 points are awarded.
	3. For every complete row of 30 that has two or more mistakes (including missing digits), 0 points are awarded.
	4. **For the last row only:** If the last row is incomplete (e.g., only the first 19 numbers have been written down) and all of the digits are correct, then the points awarded will equal the number of digits recalled (19 in this example).
	5. If the last row is incomplete and there is a single mistake (this includes a missing digit), then the points awarded will equal half the number of digits recalled. (For an odd number of digits the fraction is rounded up, e.g., for 19 the score would be 19/2 rounded up equals 10.)
	6. The winner of the event is the contestant with the highest score.

	Names and Faces
Event Title	
Aim	To commit to memory and recall as many names as possible and link them to the right face.
Time to Memorize	15 minutes
Time to Recall	30 minutes
Question Paper	1. 99 color photographs of different people (head and shoulder shots) with a first name and second name written underneath each picture. 2. Pictures are provided 9 to a page in 3 rows of 3 photographs on 10 sheets of A4 paper.
Answer Paper	1. Contestants will be given the 99 color photographs again (9 to a page in 3 rows of 3) but without the names and in a different order from that on the question sheet. 2. Contestants must clearly write down the correct name (first name and/or second name) under each photograph.
Scoring	1. A point is awarded for every correctly spelled first name.

Event Title	Names and Faces (continued)
Scoring (continued)	2. A point is awarded for every correctly spelled second name.
	3. Half a point is awarded for every first name that is phonetically correct but incorrectly spelled (e.g., Clare instead of Claire).
	4. Half a point is awarded for every second name that is phonetically correct but incorrectly spelled (e.g., Smyth instead of Smith).
	5. Points are still awarded if only the first name or the surname can be recalled.
	6. The contestant with the highest score wins.

Event Title	Speed Numbers
Aim	To commit to memory as many random digits (1, 3, 5, 8, 2, 5, etc.) as possible and recall them perfectly.
Time to Memorize	5 minutes
Time to Recall	15 minutes
Question Paper	1. Computer-generated numbers are presented in rows of 40 digits with 25 rows per page. 2. 1000 digits (1 sheet) are presented.
Answer Paper	1. Contestants must write their recalled numbers in rows of 40 digits. 2. Contestants may use the answer sheets provided or their own (as long as it has been cleared by the adjudicator before recall commences). 3. It must be clear how the rows presented on the answer paper relate to the rows on the question paper (missing rows must be clearly indicated).
Scoring	1. 40 points are awarded for every complete row that is correctly recalled in order. 2. For every complete row of 40 that has a single mistake

Event Title	Speed Numbers (continued)
Scoring (continued)	in it (this includes a missing digit), 20 points are awarded for that row.
	3. For every complete row of 40 that has two or more mistakes (including missing digits), 0 points are awarded for that row.
	4. **For the last row only:** If the last row is incomplete (e.g., only the first 29 numbers have been written down) and all of the digits are correct, then the points awarded will equal the number of digits recalled (29 in this example).
	5. If the last row is incomplete and there is a single mistake (this includes a missing digit), then the points awarded will equal half the number of digits recalled. (For an odd number of digits the fraction is rounded up, e.g., for 29, the score would be 29/2 rounded up equals 15.)
	6. For two or more mistakes in the last row (including missing digits), 0 points are awarded for that row.
	7. The winner of the event is the contestant with the highest score (the best score from the two attempts is put forward).

One-Hour Cards	
Event Title	
Aim	To commit to memory and recall as many separate packs (decks) of 52 playing cards as possible.
Time to Memorize	60 minutes
Time to Recall	120 minutes (there is a 15-minute break between memorizing and recall to allow for the collection of the packs of cards)
Question Paper	1. A number (specified by the contestant) of separate and individual shuffled packs (decks) of 52 playing cards. 2. Contestants submit the number of completely memorized packs and indicate if the last pack has only been partially committed to memory. 3. Contestants must make it clear to the adjudicators the number (order) of each pack of cards when they are handed in after being committed to memory. 4. The cards can be looked at repeatedly and more than one card can be looked at simultaneously. 5. The packs must be numbered in sequence, initialed, and bound with an elastic band. The order of

Event Title	One-Hour Cards (continued)
Question Paper (continued)	memorization (top to bottom or bottom to top) should also be indicated. This can be done during memorization or immediately after. Elastic bands and Post-it notes will be provided to the competitor for this purpose.
Answer Paper	1. Contestants must write down the order of each pack of cards so that the value (e.g., A, 2, 3 . . . J, Q, K) and suit (♣ ♦ ♥ ♠/C, D, H, S) are clear for each card in each pack.
	2. Contestants must make clear on their answer sheets to which pack the list of cards is referring.
Scoring	1. 52 points are awarded for every pack (deck) correctly recalled.
	2. 26 points are awarded if there is a single mistake in a pack.
	3. 0 points are awarded if there are two or more mistakes.
	4. **For the last pack only:** If the last pack is incomplete

Event Title	One-Hour Cards (continued)
Scoring (continued)	(e.g., only the first 38 cards were memorized) and all of the cards recalled are correct, then the points awarded will equal the number of cards recalled (38 in this example). 5. If the last pack is incomplete and there is one mistake then the points awarded will equal half the number of cards recalled. (For an odd number of cards the fraction is rounded up, e.g., for 19 cards and one mistake, the score would be 19/2 rounded up equals 10.) 6. Two or more mistakes in the last pack scores 0. 7. The winner of the event is the contestant with the highest number of points.

Event Title	Random Words
Aim	To commit to memory and recall as many random words as possible.
Time to Memorize	15 minutes
Time to Recall	30 minutes
Question Paper	1. A list of words organized in columns of 20 with 5 columns to a page. 2. 4 pages of words (400) are provided. 3. Contestants must start at the first word of column 1 and remember as many of the words as possible.
Answer Paper	1. Contestants must write down the list of words on the paper provided. 2. Contestants may use blank paper if they wish, but each word must be clearly numbered and the start and finish of each column of words easily identifiable.
Scoring	1. A point is awarded for every word in a complete column where all 20 words are correctly spelled. 2. One mistake (including any gaps) in a column of 20 words gives a score of 10 for that column (20/2).

Event Title	Random Words (continued)
Scoring (continued)	3. Two or more mistakes (including any gaps) in a column of 20 words scores 0 for that column. 4. **For the final column only:** If the final column is partially complete, a point is awarded for each word if every one is correctly spelled. 5. If the final column is partially complete, one mistake (including any gaps) in the partial column means the points awarded will equal half the number of words recalled. (For an odd number of words, the fraction is rounded up, e.g., for 19 words and one mistake, the score would be 19/2 rounded up equals 10.) 6. Two or more mistakes (including any gaps) will score 0 for the column. 7. *If a word/expression has been clearly memorized, i.e., *the main structure* clearly resembles the word to be memorized, but has been spelled in an incorrect way, no points are given for this word. It will not, however, cancel other words in a column. For example, if somebody writes "rythm" instead of "rhythm," no points will be

Event Title	Random Words (continued)
Scoring (continued)	given for this word, and, if all other words in the column are correct, full marks minus one will be given for that column (e.g., 19).

*This rule has been introduced to limit the complications that may arise from spelling ambiguities, autographical mistakes in translations, dyslexia, and handicaps for foreigners, etc.

Event Title	1-Hour Numbers
Aim	To commit to memory as many random digits (1, 3, 5, 8, 2, 5, etc.) as possible and recall them perfectly.
Time to Memorize	60 minutes
Time to Recall	120 minutes
Question Paper	1. Computer-generated numbers are presented in rows of 40 digits with 25 rows per page.
	2. 4,000 digits (4 sheets) are presented, although more are available from the adjudicator, but this must be requested one month in advance of the competition.
Answer Paper	1. Contestants must write their recalled numbers in rows of 40 digits.
	2. Contestants may use the answer sheets provided or their own (as long as it has been cleared by the adjudicator before recall commences).
	3. It must be clear how the rows presented on the answer paper relate to the rows on the question paper (missing rows must be clearly indicated).

Event Title	1-Hour Numbers (continued)
Scoring	1. 40 points are awarded for every complete row that is correctly recalled in order.
	2. For every complete row of 40 that has a single mistake in it (this includes a missing digit), 20 points are awarded for that row.
	3. For every complete row of 40 that has two or more mistakes (including missing digits), 0 points are awarded for that row.
	4. **For the last row only:** If the last row is incomplete (e.g., only the first 29 numbers have been written down) and all of the digits are correct, then the points awarded will equal the number of digits recalled (29 in this example).
	5. If the last row is incomplete and there is a single mistake (this includes a missing digit), then the points awarded will equal half the number of digits recalled. (For an odd number of digits the fraction is rounded up, e.g., for 29 the score would be 29/2 rounded up, e.g., for 29 the score would be 29/2 rounded up equals 15.)

Event Title	1-Hour Numbers (continued)
Scoring (continued)	6. For two or more mistakes in the last row (including missing digits), 0 points are awarded for the last row. 7. The winner of the event is the contestant with the highest score.

Event Title	Historic/Future Dates
Aim	To commit to memory and recall as many fictional numerical historic/future dates as possible and link them to the right historic event.
Time to Memorize	5 minutes
Time to Recall	15 minutes
Question Paper	1. 80 different historic dates with 40 dates on a page will be given.
	2. The historic dates lie between the years 1000 and 2099.
	3. All historic dates are fictitious or general (e.g., peace treaty signed).
	4. The length of the event text is between 1 and 5 words.
	5. Statistically the whole range of years will be used and no year (and no event) will be presented twice.
	6. The 4-digit number of the historic years are on the left side of the event and the events are written down under each other.

Event Title	Historic/Future Dates (continued)
Answer Paper	1. Contestants will be given 2 sheets of paper with 40 historic event texts written on each.
	2. The historic event texts are in a different order from that of the memorizing phase.
	3. Contestants must now write down the correct year in front of the event texts.
Scoring	1. A point is awarded for every correctly assigned year. All 4 digits of the year written down must be correct.
	2. No point is given for a correct year which was not assigned to the corresponding event.
	3. No minus points are given.
	4. Only one year can be written down in front of the event.
	5. The points are added up (max. 80 points) and the contestant with the highest score wins.

Spoken Numbers

Event Title	
Aim	To commit to memory and recall as many spoken numbers as possible.
Time to Memorize	Attempt 1–100 seconds Attempt 2–200 seconds Attempt 3–300 seconds
Time to Recall	Attempt 1–5 minutes Attempt 2–10 minutes Attempt 3–15 minutes
Question Paper	1. A recorded tape is played that has a clear voice reading out decimal digits in English (1, 5, 4, 8, etc.) at a rate of 1 second per digit. 2. Attempt 1–100 digits are spoken. 3. Attempt 2–200 digits are spoken. 4. Attempt 3–300 digits are spoken. 5. No writing is allowed during the playing of the tape. 6. When a contestant has reached their limit that they can memorize, they must stay in their seats, be quiet, and sit still for the remainder of the tape.

Event Title	Spoken Numbers (continued)
Question Paper (continued)	7. If for some reason the attempt has to be paused due to an external distraction, the attempt will be continued from 5 numbers before the interruption.
Answer Paper	1. Contestants must write their recalled numbers in consecutive order from the start of the spoken sequence.
	2. Contestants may use blank paper, the answer sheets provided, or their own (as long as it has been cleared by the adjudicator before recall commences).
Scoring	1. One point is awarded for every correct consecutive digit that the contestant writes down from the first digit of the spoken sequence.
	2. As soon as the contestant makes their first mistake, that is where the marking stops.
	3. For example, if a contestant recalls 127 digits but makes a mistake at the 43rd digit, then the score will be 42. If a contestant recalled 400 digits but made a mistake on the first digit, the score would be 0.
	4. The winner of the event is the contestant with the highest score.

Event Title	Speed Cards
Aim	To commit to memory and recall a single pack (deck) of 52 playing cards in the shortest possible time.
Time to Memorize	5 minutes (there are two attempts at this event, with a new deck each time)
Time to Recall	5 minutes (for each attempt)
Question Paper	1. A freshly shuffled pack (deck) of 52 playing cards. 2. Contestants who expect to memorize the complete pack (deck) of cards in less than 5 minutes must inform the adjudicator so that a timekeeper with a stopwatch can be assigned. 3. Contestants must not begin recalling their pack until either the adjudicator has announced that the 5-minute period is complete or all of the contestants have finished memorizing within the 5-minute limit. 4. Contestants who expect to complete their memorization in less than 5 minutes must agree with their invigilator an appropriate signal that indicates they have finished memorizing.

Event Title	Speed Cards (continued)
Question Paper (continued)	5. The cards can be looked at repeatedly and more than one card can be looked at simultaneously.
Answer Paper	1. After the memorizing phase each contestant gets a **second pack of cards** which is in perfect order (i.e., 2 ♦ 3 ♦ 4 ♦ etc.). The contestant has to order this second deck of cards in the same sequence as the pack just memorized. 2. After the recall phase both decks will be put beside each other on the table, the top card being the first one memorized.
Scoring	1. The arbiter will compare each card from the memorized pack with each card of the recall pack. At the first discrepancy between the two packs, only the cards up to this point will be counted. 2. The contestant who memorizes all 52 cards in the quickest time and correctly recalls the pack, wins the event. 3. Points will be awarded only if the entire pack has

Event Title	**Speed Cards** (continued)
Scoring (continued)	been correctly recalled. 4. The best score from the two attempts will count.

Acknowledgments

For what began as a lump in my throat that migrated into a story and then into this book, I have many to thank. Dr. Tinsley Rucker, whose thoroughness immediately diagnosed my thyroid problem. Dr. James Thomas, whose skillful hands delicately removed the tumor. Dr. Joseph Moore and his colleagues at Duke University Medical Center for eradicating the malignancy. Dr. Joseph Maldjian, Dr. Paul Laurienti, Dr. Jonathan Burdette, and the staff of the Advanced Neuroscience Imaging Research Lab at Wake Forest University Baptist Medical Center for their passion for the brain and their generosity in sharing their time, equipment, and results. Tony Buzan, my mentor and friend, whose gifts of knowledge and enlightenment are beyond my capacity to repay. Tony Dottino and his team, who established the USA National Memory Championships as a way of showcasing the extraordinary power of the developed memory.

This book would not have been possible without my literary agent, Jodie Rhodes. I thank Free Press, which had the willingness to invest in me, and specifically my editor, Fred Hills, and his assistant, Kirsa Rein, who have so graciously shared their wisdom and encouragement throughout this project. I am grateful to writer Doug Sease for sharing his craft of structure and style. I have learned so much.

Finally, I'd like to thank my parents, Charles and Jane Hagwood, my daughter, Kristen, and all of my friends for their endless support during my illness and the writing of this book; and most especially my wife, Janet, whose love for me is a living example of God's grace.

About the Author

Scott Hagwood was born in Asheville, North Carolina, and raised near Knoxville, Tennessee. After struggling for years with memory problems, he developed the mental exercises that made him the first American Grand Master of Memory. Hagwood worked for several years as a chemical consultant doing risk analysis for Fortune 500 companies. He is married with a daughter and lives in Fayetteville, North Carolina.

The employees of Thorndike Press hope you have enjoyed this Large Print book. All our Thorndike and Wheeler Large Print titles are designed for easy reading, and all our books are made to last. Other Thorndike Press Large Print books are available at your library, through selected bookstores, or directly from us.

For information about titles, please call:

(800) 223-1244

or visit our Web site at:

www.gale.com/thorndike
www.gale.com/wheeler

To share your comments, please write:

Publisher
Thorndike Press
295 Kennedy Memorial Drive
Waterville, ME   04901